THE BRITISH LIBRARY
writers' lives

Jane Austen

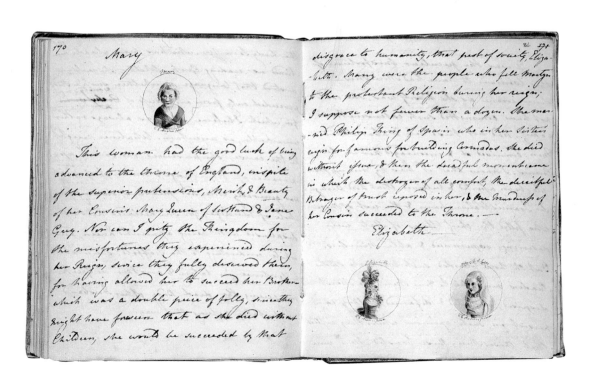

Chawton, July 26. – 1809.

My dearest Frank, I wish you joy
Of Mary's safety with a Boy,
Whose birth has given little pain
Compared with that of Mary Jane. –
May he a growing Blessing prove,
And well deserve his Parents' Love! –
Endow'd with Art's & Nature's Good,
Thy name possessing with thy Blood,
In him, in all his ways, may we
Another Francis William see! –
Thy infant days may he inherit,
Thy warmth, nay insolence of spirit; –
We would not with one fault dispense
To weaken the resemblance.
May he revive thy Nursery sin,
Peeping as daringly within,
His curly Locks but just descried,
With "Bet, my be not come to bide." –
Fearless of danger, braving pain,
And threaten'd very oft in vain,
Still may one Terror daunt his Soul,
One needful engine of Controul

THE BRITISH LIBRARY
writers' lives

Jane Austen

DEIRDRE LE FAYE

OXFORD UNIVERSITY PRESS
New York

This unsigned painting
of Steventon Parsonage
was taken from a
scrap book which was
made by James Edward
Austen-Leigh for the
amusement of his
children. It is now in
the possession of Joan
Austen-Leigh by whose
permission it is used.

≋ Contents

≋ *Introduction*

On Monday 21 July 1817 *The Hampshire Chronicle and Courier*, published in Winchester and circulating in a wide radius throughout the south of England, offered its readers the usual compilation of the past week's events. Since the ending of the war with France in 1815, there was nowadays very little foreign news, as the editor admitted - the Duchesse de Berri had given birth to a daughter who had died two days later, and there were still difficulties in reducing the size of the Army of Occupation. Information reprinted from the London papers included the enviable statement that Earl Grosvenor was likely to obtain an addition of at least £20,000 a year to his already large income, by the recent discovery of a fine lead mine on his estates in North Wales; the export trade from Newcastle on Tyne was flourishing; and William Cobbett, the Radical journalist, had published an article on the subject of emigration to America, warning English farmworkers that although they might eventually succeed in making a very prosperous living for themselves, they must bear in mind the cost of the voyage out and the risks of homesickness and unemployment.

Nearer home, in the neighbouring county of Wiltshire several marriages and deaths were recorded, the latter including those of Miss Whittaker, at an advanced age after a short illness, and Miss Edgell of Trowbridge, aged 18. In Hampshire, HMS *Larkins* was lying in Portsmouth harbour with 250 convicts on board, and would soon set sail for a fast non-stop three-month voyage transporting them to the penal settlement in New South Wales, Australia. Troopships had returned from the West Indies with many soldiers sick, and so were now anchored under quarantine outside the harbour. The officers of HMS *Queen Charlotte* had 'handsomely entertained a numerous circle of friends. The play of *A Cure for the Heart-ache*, and the afterpiece of *The Mock Doctor*, were got up with great effect and elegance, and the characters throughout were supported in a spirited manner. A Ball succeeded, which was continued till daylight'. There was very little news from Winchester itself – prices for grain were steady or declining, several members of the gentry had sent subscriptions for the benefit of the Female Asylum, a concert held at St John's House had been 'honoured with the presence of a numerous and genteel

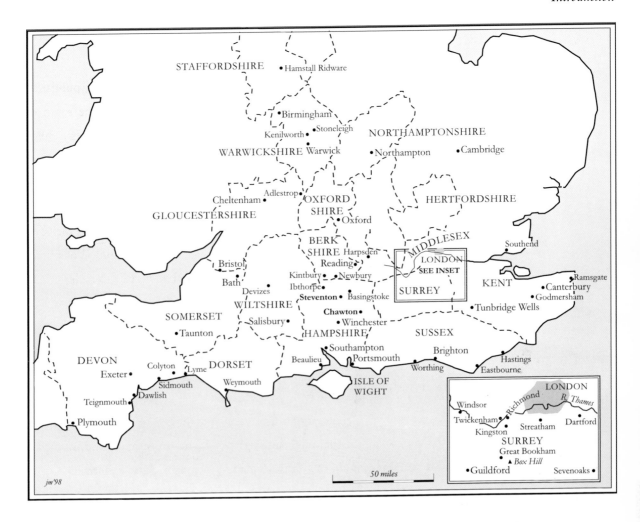

STAFFORDSHIRE • Hamstall Ridware

•Birmingham

Kenilworth •Stoneleigh NORTHAMPTONSHIRE

WARWICKSHIRE Warwick •Northampton •Cambridge

Adlestrop• OXFORD HERTFORDSHIRE
Cheltenham • SHIRE
GLOUCESTERSHIRE •Oxford

BERK MIDDLESEX Southend
SHIRE Harpsden LONDON
•Bristol Reading• SEE INSET
Bath Kintbury •Newbury SURREY KENT Ramsgate
Devizes Ibthorpe • •Canterbury
WILTSHIRE **Steventon** • Basingstoke •Godmersham
•Chawton •Tunbridge Wells
SOMERSET •Winchester
•Salisbury HAMPSHIRE SUSSEX
•Taunton
DEVON DORSET Southampton Brighton Hastings
Colyton Beaulieu •Portsmouth Worthing Eastbourne
Exeter• •Lyme Weymouth ISLE OF
Sidmouth WIGHT
Teignmouth •Dawlish
•Plymouth

jm'98 50 miles

LONDON
Windsor R. *Thames*
Twickenham• Streatham Dartford
Kingston
SURREY
Great Bookham
▲ *Box Hill*
•Guildford Sevenoaks •

assemblage'; and: 'Died, yesterday, in College-street, Miss Jane Austen, youngest daughter of the late Rev George Austen, formerly Rector of Steventon, in this county'.

The Hampshire Chronicle had nothing further to say on the subject, and for the editor this Miss Austen was no doubt as obscure and unremarkable as Miss Whittaker or Miss Edgell, her name and death as likely to be instantly forgotten by his readers. It was left to a later obituary, in the *New Monthly Magazine* for September 1817, to add an explanatory note: 'She was the ingenious authoress of the novels entitled *Emma*, *Mansfield Park*, *Pride and Prejudice*, and *Sense and Sensibility*'.

Jane Austen is now one of the most popular novelists in the English language, and yet on the face of it one of the most unlikely candidates for such a title.

Map of Southern England, showing places known to Jane Austen or mentioned in her writings.

7

Watercolour sketch of Jane Austen by her sister Cassandra, probably made c.1810. This is the only authentic representation of Jane's features, and shows a strong family resemblance to her father and brothers.

National Portrait Gallery, London.

Steel engraving after the sketch, used as frontispiece to the Memoir of Jane Austen in 1870. Those of Jane's older nieces who were still alive considered it gave a reasonable representation of her features as they remembered her.

She was the younger daughter of a not-very-well off country clergyman, never married, never lived outside her own family circle, did not travel abroad – indeed, did not move beyond the southern half of England – and died at the age of 41, leaving behind only six completed novels. Yet her works have never been out of print, and in this century, within the last three decades in particular, never a year passes without some fresh adaptation of her stories for stage, screen, or television. Numerous modern biographies have been and still are being written, despite the fact that her quiet and uneventful short life is seriously lacking in firm documentary evidence. She did not write any autobiographical memoirs or reminiscences, did not keep a journal, and had no Boswell to record her actions and conversations; and as she did not move in the highest social circles her name does not appear in the correspondence or memoirs of the nobility of the period. She published her novels anonymously – the first, *Sense and Sensibility*, was 'By A Lady', and the later ones were 'By the Author of [one of her previous novels]' – and although as a result of their growing popularity her identity did eventually become known and a little curiosity was aroused amongst some of her readers, no contemporary biography was ever

called for or written. When her brother
Henry undertook the posthumous publication
of her last two novels, *Northanger Abbey* and
Persuasion, in 1818, he prefaced them with
only the briefest of biographical comments,
and for many years thereafter this limited
information had to suffice.

There is likewise a sad lack of visual
evidence available; no professional portrait
was ever painted of Jane, and the only
authentic representation of her is the
watercolour sketch drawn by her sister
Cassandra, probably about 1810, which is now
in the National Portrait Gallery, London.
This is accurate in so far as it shows a strong
family likeness to her father and brothers, of
whom professional portraits were painted at
various dates, but is otherwise admittedly

*Watercolour sketch of
Jane, made by
Cassandra in the
summer of 1804.*

Private collection.

amateurish. An engraved version of Cassandra's sketch was made in 1869, and this is
the one usually reproduced in biographies, sometimes with unwarranted additions of
furniture and clothing to turn it into a half-length instead of a bust portrait.   During
one of their summer holidays in 1804, Cassandra also drew a watercolour sketch of
Jane 'sitting down out of doors, on a hot day, with her bonnet-strings untied', as their
niece Anna afterwards described it – but this is only a back view and does not show
Jane's face.   The National Portrait Gallery has in addition a silhouette which may
quite possibly show Jane in her younger days, but it seems unlikely that complete
proof of this will ever be forthcoming.

The story of Jane's life must therefore be reconstructed from elements of her
personal knowledge which can be identified through close study of her novels, and
from some surviving letters from her (about 160, most of which are to her sister
Cassandra), miscellaneous references to her in other family correspondence and
diaries, and oral tradition passed down from the nephews and nieces who knew her

L'aimable Jane:
a silhouette found in
1944, pasted into Vol. II
of the second edition
(1816) of Mansfield Park,
and so presumed to be of
Jane Austen.
It seems to show a young
woman, and so may have
been made in Bath by
Mrs Collins around
1795.

National Portrait Gallery,
London

Opening page of the
Memoir of Jane Austen
by Jane's nephew, Revd
James Edward Austen-
Leigh, 1869-70; this
was her first biography,
with information
provided by those who
knew her.

A MEMOIR

OF

JANE AUSTEN.

CHAPTER I.

Introductory Remarks—Birth of Jane Austen—Her Family
Connections—Their Influence on her Writings.

 ORE than half a century has passed away
since I, the youngest of the mourners,*
attended the funeral of my dear aunt
Jane in Winchester Cathedral ; and now,
in my old age, I am asked whether my memory
will serve to rescue from oblivion any events of her
life or any traits of her character to satisfy the enquiries of a generation of readers who have been
born since she died. Of events her life was singularly barren: few changes and no great crisis ever
broke the smooth current of its course. Even her
fame may be said to have been posthumous: it did

* I went to represent my father, who was too unwell to attend himself, and thus I was the only one of my generation present.

B

best.   It may be that in the future further letters will come to light, or full diaries kept by someone who knew her well, but for the present all biographers have nothing but these sources to study and interpret.   Luckily, it was part of Jane Austen's deliberate technique to create utterly accurate contemporary settings for her novels, so that although she herself may remain a tantalisingly elusive personality, always a little bit beyond camera range, as it were – and not unlike Shakespeare, too, in this respect – we can at least get a clear picture from her writings of the world with which she was familiar, and this bright background then assists in defining her shadowy image when the latter is superimposed upon it.

Steventon

Family and Birth

When Jane Austen was born at Steventon rectory, on the frosty night of Saturday 16 December 1775, she entered the world as the seventh child and second daughter of the Revd George Austen, rector of the two little adjoining rural parishes of Steventon and Deane in north-east Hampshire. Mr Austen sent the news to his sister-in-law Mrs Walter the next morning: '... last night the time came, and without a great deal of warning, everything was soon happily over. We have now another girl, a present plaything for her sister Cassy and a future companion. She is to be Jenny, and seems to me as if she would be as like Henry, as Cassy is to Neddy. Your sister thank God is pure well after it, and sends her love to you and my brother ...' Mr Austen's very first comment on his new daughter, linking her already to her fourth brother in looks and to her only sister in affection, proved a most accurate prediction. Jane's resemblance to Henry persisted in later life, and her sisterly companionship with Cassandra was so close that even years after Jane's death Cassandra still spoke of her with 'an accent of *living* love in her voice'.

Jane's immediate ancestry was not, however, rooted in Hampshire, as her parents came from Kent and Oxfordshire respectively. The Revd George Austen was a member of the long-established and widespread family of Austens, sheep-farming yeomen in Kent who were rising into gentility by reason of the wealth gained from the local woollen industry. George himself had been orphaned early in life, but thanks to the support of his rich uncle Francis Austen, an eminently successful solicitor in Sevenoaks, Kent, he had been able to study at St John's College, Oxford, and go on to take Holy Orders. Another Kentish connection, his cousin-by-marriage Mr Thomas Broadnax May Knight, had appointed him as rector of Steventon parish; a few years later Mr Francis Austen had bought for him the adjacent living of Deane. On the combined income of these two little parishes, plus some fees gained by tutoring boys for university entrance, and the produce of his rectory farm, Mr Austen and his wife were able to rear their eight children in reasonable comfort though never in luxury.

Mrs Austen, formerly Cassandra Leigh, was the daughter of the rector of Harpsden, near Henley-on-Thames, Oxfordshire. Her father, Revd Thomas Leigh, like Revd George Austen, stemmed from a junior branch of a large family, but the Leighs were of rather higher social standing than the Austens, having been landed gentry in Gloucestershire since the sixteenth century, while another branch in Warwickshire had gained a peerage for their loyalty to Charles I. They were also of a more intellectual bent than the Austens, and Mrs Austen's uncle Revd Dr Theophilus Leigh was the Master of Balliol College, Oxford, for more than fifty years. It seems probable that Cassandra Leigh met her future husband in Oxford, perhaps through the good offices of her uncle.

George Austen and Cassandra Leigh were married at Walcot church in Bath on 26 April 1764, and set off for Hampshire immediately after the wedding ceremony. For the first four years of their married life they rented Deane rectory, because Steventon rectory was dilapidated and needed repairing before it could be occupied. Mrs Austen's widowed mother came from Bath to join them for the last few years of her life, accompanied by her ward, George Hastings, who might perhaps be considered as Mr Austen's first pupil. This little boy, born in India in 1757, was the only surviving child of Warren Hastings, the future Governor General of Bengal, and, as was then the custom, had been sent back to England for education. Warren Hastings had known the Leigh family since his own childhood in England, and evidently felt they were the best friends to whom he could entrust the care of his son.

Unfortunately poor little George Hastings did not live long, even under the care of Mrs Leigh and the Austens, but died of diphtheria ('putrid sore throat') in the autumn of 1764, much to the grief of Mrs Austen. However, George Hastings's place in the household was soon filled by the births of the Austens' own three eldest sons, James, George, and Edward, before the young family moved to Steventon rectory in the summer of 1768. Here the rest of their children were born – Henry, Cassandra, Francis, Jane, and finally Charles, 'our own particular little brother', as Cassandra and Jane referred to him in later years.

Other members of Jane's family group were her uncles and aunts and their families – Mr and Mrs William Hampson Walter (her father's elder half-brother, whose daughter Philadelphia's letters provide some of the earliest references to Jane's childhood); the widowed Mrs Hancock (her father's sister, whose pretty, flirtatious daughter Eliza had an unexpectedly exciting life and brought the effects of the French Revolution straight into the quiet Steventon parsonage); Revd Dr and Mrs

Warren Hastings (1732-1818), by Sir Joshua Reynolds, 1766-68

National Portrait Gallery, London.

Above left
Francis Austen (1774-1865), miniature 1796, in the uniform of a Lieutenant.

Private collection.

Edward Cooper (her mother's sister, and their two children Edward and Jane); and Mr and Mrs James Leigh-Perrot (her mother's brother, rich but childless). The Walters had only a modest income and in consequence lived quietly in Kent, and the Austens saw them only occasionally; Mrs Hancock and the Cooper parents all died during Jane's girlhood; but Mr and Mrs Leigh-Perrot kept in close touch with the Austens and are frequently mentioned in Jane's letters in her later life, always being referred to simply as 'my Uncle' and 'my Aunt'. They lived in a small manor-house called Scarlets, near Wargrave in Berkshire, but usually spent several months of each year on holiday in Bath.

Mr Austen was a tall, thin, handsome man, with peculiarly bright hazel eyes and chestnut brown hair which turned milky white in later life, gentle and scholarly and devoted to his family and his parishioners. Mrs Austen was small and thin, with dark hair, grey eyes and a beakily aristocratic nose; she was brisk, active and quick-witted, with plenty of sparkle and spirit in her talk. Jane and her siblings were lucky to inherit these parental characteristics, as they were all thin, healthy and active, and highly intelligent. Henry and Charles were both remarkably tall and good-looking, with their father's colouring, Edward and Frank were small like their mother, James and Cassandra seem to have been medium in height and with their mother's colouring, and Jane herself was tall and slender with her father's hazel eyes and chestnut brown hair. The only unlucky child in the family was George junior, the second son; there are references in early family letters to the epileptic fits he suffered, and it seems possible he was also deaf and dumb. Mrs Austen tried to rear him at home, but with seven other children as well as her husband's pupils to look after, she evidently found the task impossible. In accordance with the custom of the period, therefore, George was boarded out locally at the little village of Monk Sherborne with a respectable cottager family as his foster-parents, and his father and later his brothers paid for his upkeep and maintained contact with him until his peaceful death many years later.

The present-day village of Steventon has changed considerably over the last two centuries, and probably the only building surviving from Jane's day is the ancient little church of St Nicholas. In the eighteenth century the medieval and Tudor buildings of Steventon manor-house and its home farm were opposite the church,

and the rectory was about half a mile away downhill.   It stood at the corner of the small lane that led to the church and the slightly bigger lane that led to the village of Deane, in a shallow valley, surrounded by sloping meadows dotted with tall elm trees, and with a few cottages close by at the road junction.   The rectory was not a particularly handsome or well-built house – it seems to have had low-ceilinged rooms lit by small casement windows, and whitewashed brick walls with a red tile roof, like many other local houses of the time – but it was large enough to be

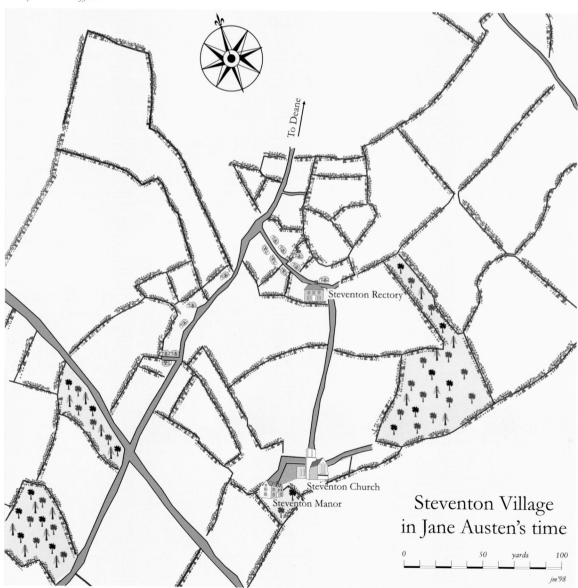

To Deane

Steventon Rectory

Steventon Church

Steventon Manor

Steventon Village in Jane Austen's time

0   50   *yards*   100

jm'98

comfortable for Mr Austen and his family and pupils, with seven bedrooms and three attics above the living rooms and kitchens. At the back of the house, on the warm southern side and overlooking the walled garden with its strawberry beds, grassy walk, and sundial, Mr Austen had his bow-windowed study; Mrs Austen used the well-lit entrance parlour at the front of the house as her sewing-room, constantly making or repairing the family's clothes. This was Jane's home for the first twenty-five years of her life.

Steventon church as it is today; the spire was added in the last century, after Jane's time.

By kind permission of the Rector and Churchwardens.

Cottages at Steventon (now no longer existing); watercolour probably by Anna Lefroy, c.1810.

Jane Austen Memorial Trust.

Glebe plan of 1821, showing the layout of Steventon rectory with its carriage-drive, garden, yard, and fields, at the time Henry Austen was living there.

Jane Austen Memorial Trust.

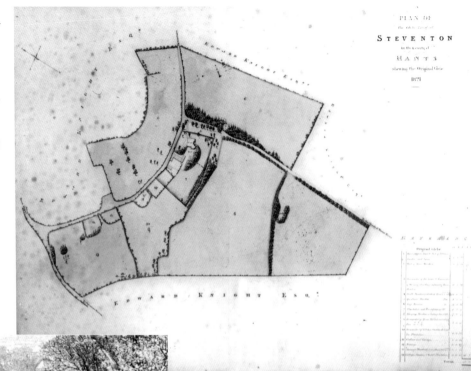

Front view of Steventon Rectory: a wood engraving by George Pearson after a drawing by E.M. Wimperis, as used in the Memoir *of 1870.*

Schooling

At the end of the eighteenth century it was usual for gentry families to send their sons away to school but to keep their daughters at home, taught by their mother or governess. The Austens, however, reversed this procedure, presumably because Mr Austen realised he would not be able to afford the expense of keeping five sons at boarding school. He himself therefore taught his sons at home, and from 1773 until 1796 took in a succession of pupils, chosen from the families of his old university friends, to be their classmates and also to provide fees to enhance the rectory finances. Not all the names of these pupils have been recorded, but the four Fowle boys, sons of the vicar of Kintbury in Berkshire, became lifelong friends of the Austens. In the meantime, Cassandra and little Jane, with their cousin Jane Cooper, were sent away to Oxford in the spring of 1783 to be tutored at home by Mrs Cawley, who was the sister of the Revd Dr Cooper and also the widow of the Principal of

Brasenose College, Oxford.   Later in 1783 Mrs Cawley moved to Southampton, taking the little girls with her, and here Jane Austen's life nearly came to a premature end.   In August 1783 soldiers returning from Gibraltar were quartered in the town and brought with them typhus ('putrid') fever as a result of their insanitary conditions during the voyage home. The infection rapidly spread, and both Cassandra and Jane fell ill.   Mrs Cawley did not think they were sufficiently ill to warrant informing their parents, but luckily Jane Cooper, as the eldest of the three, took it upon herself to write home for help.   Mrs Austen and Mrs Cooper at once set off to retrieve their children; family tradition recalled that Jane Austen was very ill and nearly died, and tragically Mrs Cooper herself caught the fever and died a few weeks later.

It was not until the spring of 1785 that the Austens tried again to send their daughters away, this time choosing Mrs La Tournelle's Ladies Boarding School in Reading, Berkshire, a large establishment with forty or more pupils, which was well-known throughout the south of England for providing a sensible and practical education for the daughters of the gentry and professional classes.   It was sometimes

Reading Abbey Gateway in the eighteenth century; Mrs La Tournelle's school occupied the large house on the left of the picture. The gateway still survives, flanked now by modern office development.

Museum of Reading.

referred to as the Abbey House school, from the fact that its premises were in a large old red-brick house built adjoining the inner gateway of what had once been the enormous Reading Abbey, but of which only a few walls still remained standing

*A page from
Goody Two Shoes;
one of the very few
surviving of Jane's
childhood books, with her
name written at the top
of the page.*

Private collection.

following its dissolution in the days of Henry VIII. Originally the Austens had planned that only Cassandra should go to Reading, as Jane was still too young to make her going to school at all necessary; but Jane could not bear the idea of being separated from her sister – 'if Cassandra's head had been going to be cut off, Jane would have hers cut off too' – was how Mrs Austen remembered it; so as the Austens were kind and understanding parents, Jane had her way and accompanied Cassandra to Reading. The girls were happy here, with the domestic life of the school well-managed by the stout old Mrs La Tournelle, while the lessons and hours of study were not exacting, so that there was plenty of time to play with the other pupils in the large garden that overlooked the ivy-grown ruins of the Abbey. It was possible for girls to stay on at the Abbey House until well into their teens, but it seems that the Austens soon found they could not after all afford to keep both their daughters there for so many years – Mrs La Tournelle charged about £35 a year for each pupil – and the girls returned home for good to Steventon before Christmas 1786. These two brief scholastic ventures were the only times Jane ever lived away from home, and for the rest of her life she remained within her immediate family circle.

'Your outlandish cousin'

A surprisingly flamboyant member of the Austen family was Mr Austen's niece Eliza, only child of his elder sister Philadelphia; the latter, being a penniless orphan, had had a voyage to India paid for by her wealthy uncle, Mr Francis Austen of Sevenoaks, in the expectation she would find a husband amongst the lonely European employees of the East India Company at their trading station in the growing city of Calcutta. Philadelphia had arrived in India in 1752 and indeed within a few months had married Tysoe Saul Hancock, employed by the East India Company as a surgeon. It may be that the match was in fact pre-arranged, as Francis Austen acted as Mr Hancock's attorney or agent for monies transmitted back to England. The Hancocks had one daughter, and asked Warren Hastings, an old friend and business partner of Mr Hancock, to be her godfather. She was therefore named in memory of Hastings's own daughter Elizabeth, who had died at the age of only three weeks. Mr Hancock, in addition to his medical duties, attempted various mercantile ventures, and with the profits from these the family returned to England in 1765, hoping to invest the capital and live off dividends. However, after only a couple of years it became clear that their funds were insufficient for their chosen lifestyle, and Mr Hancock returned alone to India in 1768 with the anticipation of making a second fortune. Unfortunately he was by now in poor health, and whether it was due to his frequent illnesses or just bad luck, all his ventures seemed to fail and so far from amassing capital he ran further and further into debt. Warren Hastings, on the other hand, continued to rise in the world, and with the generosity towards his friends for which he became famed in later life, set up a trust fund for his god-daughter that would provide an income of about £400 a year for life. Had it not been for this, Eliza and her mother would have found themselves practically in poverty following Mr Hancock's death.

Left: Jane's aunt, Philadelphia Austen (1730-92), later Mrs Hancock; a miniature by John Smart, c.1768, set in diamonds.

Jane Austen Memorial Trust.

Right: Jane's cousin/sister-in-law Eliza Hancock (1761-1813), later Mme. de Feuillide and secondly Mrs Henry Austen. Miniature by unknown French artist, 1780.

Private collection.

After Mr Hancock's return to India, his wife and daughter lived in London, renting houses in the smart newly-developing Marylebone district north of Oxford Street. Here, as her father specifically requested his wife in his letters home, Eliza had the best possible tuition in music and dancing, writing and arithmetic from visiting masters, such knowledge then being considered indispensable for any girl who hoped to marry into good society. He was also anxious that she should speak French well – this was another elegant accomplishment – so after the news of his death in Calcutta in 1775 had been received in London and his tangled debts more or less sorted out, Mrs Hancock and Eliza went to the Continent in 1777. They travelled first in Germany and Belgium, and then settled in Paris in the autumn of 1779. Here they managed somehow to obtain an introduction into French high society, and Eliza, now in her late teens, was in her element. She sent a miniature home to her Austen relations, which shows her as a slender girl with large dark eyes set in a piquante little face, her frothy white dress trimmed with blue ribbons and another blue ribbon entwined in her romantically tumbled powdered curls. A group of letters from Eliza survives, written to her country-mouse cousin Philadelphia ('Phylly') Walter in Kent, talking of trips to the court at Versailles with details of the dresses worn by Queen Marie Antoinette, and giving other tantalising accounts of balls, parties and smart Parisian life. Eliza soon met a dashing young officer, Jean-François Capot de Feuillide, a Captain in the Queen's Regiment of Dragoons, with a small estate in the south of France, and they were married in 1781. They continued to live in Paris for some years, and it was not until 1784 that Eliza and her husband returned to his home at Nérac in Guienne, where he had been given a royal grant of an area of marshland provided he could drain and cultivate it. The Comte de Feuillide (as he liked to be known) was as efficient a landowner as he had been a soldier, and his works of reclamation progressed fast. Eliza became pregnant and returned to England with her mother in the summer of 1786, as she wrote to Phylly Walter: ' ... should a Son be *in store* for M de Feuillide he greatly wishes him to be a native of England for he pays me the Compliment of being very partial to my Country ...' and her son was born in London in June of that year. Eliza called him Hastings, possibly in the hope that her godfather might set up another trust fund for the baby in return for this compliment.

At Christmas 1786 Mrs Hancock, with Eliza and baby Hastings, all came to stay at Steventon rectory, and the eleven-year-old Jane first made the acquaintance of her beautiful and sophisticated elder cousin. However worldly Eliza might have become, she had no difficulty about making herself at home in rural Hampshire and playing a hired piano so that the young Austens and their visiting Cooper cousins could dance in the parlour as part of the New Year festivities. Jane's initial childish and flattering admiration for her cousin developed in later years into a steady adult friendship which lasted to the end of Eliza's life.

Amateur Dramatics

Now that the Austen children were growing up, they were able to co-operate in order to provide their own entertainment for the long winter evenings, and James, as the eldest, organised amateur theatrical performances for several Christmas holidays in succession between 1782 and 1788, writing his own versified prologues and epilogues for these productions, and seeing to it that proper scenery was constructed and painted. The plays were presented either in the rectory dining-room or else in the barn just across the lane from the house. The first play chosen was a costume drama, *Matilda*, set at the time of the Norman Conquest, but thereafter favourite comedies of the period were preferred – *The Wonder*, *The Chances*, *The Sultan*, *High Life Below Stairs*, *The Rivals* were some of them – with the young Austens and sometimes their visiting cousins to take the parts, and the audiences formed by family and friends. Eliza de Feuillide came to Steventon again for the Christmas of 1787, and played the heroine in *The Wonder*, while in the winter of 1788-89 Jane Cooper was the heroine of *The Sultan*, playing opposite Henry Austen in the title role. Jane Austen herself was probably too young to play anything but very minor parts, but her clear memories of the domestic excitement caused by these amateur theatricals enabled her, years later, to make the production of *Lovers' Vows* one of the focal events in *Mansfield Park*.

First Compositions

It was also now, following her return from school, that Jane started to write, beginning by composing the various comic short stories or essays that are referred to

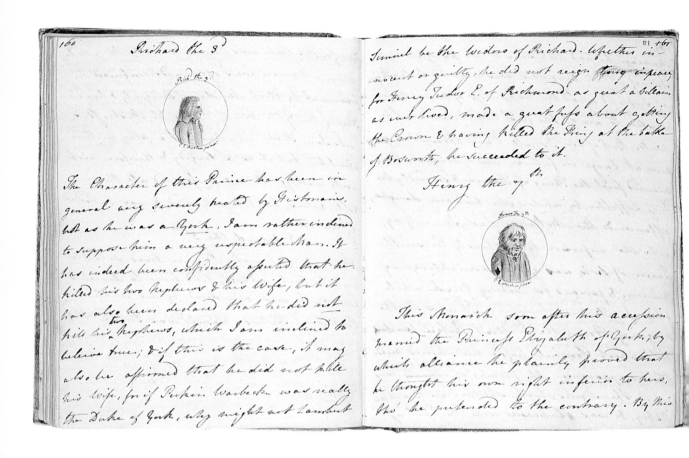

collectively as her *Juvenilia*, and of which she subsequently made fair copies in the three manuscript books known simply as 'Volume the First', 'Volume the Second', and 'Volume the Third'. Not all the pieces are dated, but they were composed between 1786 and 1793 and were evidently written for family amusement, to be read aloud round the fireside, or perhaps to be performed as part of the theatrical entertainments, as three little plays have been preserved – *The Visit*, *The Mystery*, and the fragmentary *The First Act of a Comedy*. Some of them have specific dedications to members of the family and so contain what may have been particularly appropriate references or jokes. Jane's memories of 'the stinking fish of Southampton' surface in *Love and Freindship* (her spelling was still a little uncertain), which she dedicated to Eliza de Feuillide in 1790; and in *The History of England*, written in 1791 and dedicated to Cassandra, Henry VIII is thanked for creating the romantic monastic ruins – for example at Reading, as Cassandra would recall from their schooldays –

which have been 'of infinite use to the landscape of England in general'. The earliest pieces are of course the shortest, but the later stories, especially the last two, *Evelyn* and *Catharine, or, The Bower*, are longer and already foreshadow Jane's development into a true authoress. It is a tribute to her youthful intelligence that these little squibs, parodies and burlesques are still comic in the eyes of modern readers. They are deliberately composed, with an amazingly mature appreciation for wit and irony, and display already a sense of literary style and choice of language.

The opening page of Catherine, or, The Bower, *with Jane's dedication of the story to Cassandra, from 'Volume the Third'.*

The British Library, Add.MS.65381, ff. 16v-17

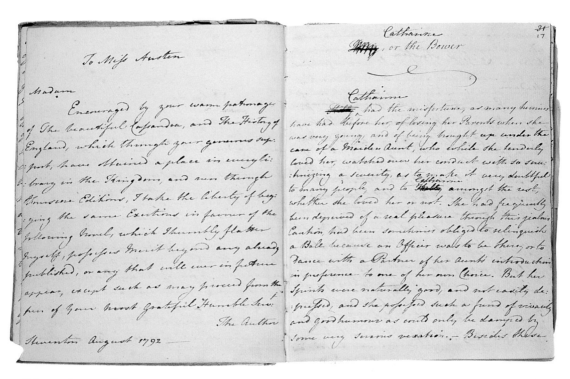

Education at home

Even though her formal schooling had ended, Jane's education continued at home, guided by her parents and eldest brother James. From her mother she learnt the practicalities of housekeeping in the country – enough arithmetic to be able to write up the domestic accounts, how to instruct and supervise servants, to plan the use of the kitchen garden, the poultry-yard and the domestic dairy – and how to sew and embroider neatly in order to make and mend clothes. In later life Cassandra and Jane were able to purchase lengths of their chosen fabrics and then pay professional dressmakers to turn these into gowns, but in the Steventon days the girls would certainly have had to make their own dresses as well as shirts and cravats for their father and brothers. She also read a great deal, and the family tradition is that James encouraged and guided her studies in this respect. Mr Austen allowed himself the luxury of buying books, and by the time the family eventually left Steventon in 1801 he had amassed a library of some 500 volumes, all of which were available for his children and pupils to read. He did not, like some clerics, disapprove of light fiction, and some of Jane's *Juvenilia* show that she was already well-acquainted with contemporary best-selling novels. She much enjoyed Richardson's *Sir Charles Grandison*, which she read over and over again until the characters were as familiar to her as if they had been living friends, and also knew Fielding's *Tom Jones* nearly as well. She was a great admirer of Dr Johnson, reading not only his own publications but also Boswell's and Mrs Piozzi's biographical works. From the authors of the past she read Shakespeare, Milton, and Pope, and amongst living authors William Cowper was her favourite poet. She also worked her way through Oliver Goldsmith's *The History of England, from the earliest times to the death of George II*, which was not particularly profound or well-written but useful for a general overview of English history. Jane by now was quite old enough to appreciate the shortcomings of Goldsmith's text, and in 1791 produced her own gleeful parody, *The History of England from the reign of Henry the 4th to the death of Charles the 1st, by a partial, prejudiced, and ignorant Historian*. Another Hampshire clergyman, the Revd William Gilpin, had made a name for himself by travelling round Britain and publishing essays on the picturesque beauties of the various counties – these came to be referred to collectively as 'Gilpin on the Picturesque' – and Jane's brother Henry remembered that she had read and admired his writings at a very early age. Gilpin's influence appears in Chapter 18 of *Sense and Sensibility*, when Edward Ferrars teases Marianne Dashwood by declaring: 'I like a fine prospect, but not on picturesque principles. I do not like crooked, twisted, blasted trees. I admire them much more if they are tall, straight and flourishing. I do not like ruined, tattered cottages. I am not fond of nettles, or thistles, or heath blossoms. I have more pleasure in a snug farm-house than a watch-tower – and a troop of tidy, happy villagers please me better than the finest banditti in the world'.

Music, singing, dancing, and some knowledge of foreign languages were also a necessary part of a girl's accomplishments, and although the Austens could not afford to buy the best instruments and hire a succession of teachers, they did manage to acquire a pianoforte in the 1790s, and the Winchester Cathedral organist, who doubled as a music-master, visited Steventon from time to time to teach Jane until at least 1796.   She learnt a little Italian, presumably in conjunction with these music lessons;   and also learnt enough French from textbooks to be able to read it satisfactorily, though apparently she could never speak it fluently.   At that period girls were not expected to study Latin or Greek, but Jane evidently picked up a good deal of classical knowledge from hearing her father teaching his sons and pupils.   Mr Austen was at one time able to pay for his children to have a few drawing lessons, and Henry in particular benefited from this tuition, being considered the artist of the family.   A few sketches by Cassandra survive – the most important, of course, being those two she did of Jane – but although Jane was quite talented too in this respect in her childhood, as she grew up she preferred to employ her time in literary composition.

Several of Jane's music books have been preserved, showing her neat copying of both vocal and instrumental music.

Jane Austen Memorial Trust.

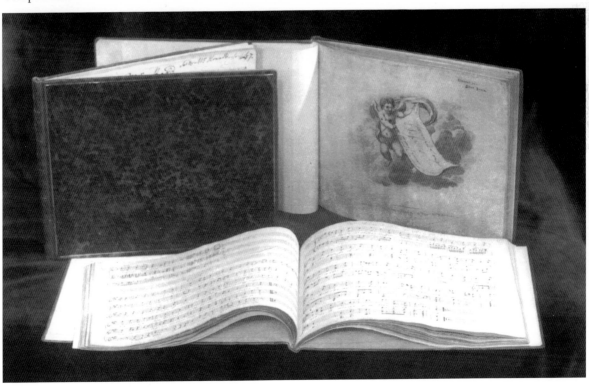

≋ *Wider Circles*

Growing up at Steventon

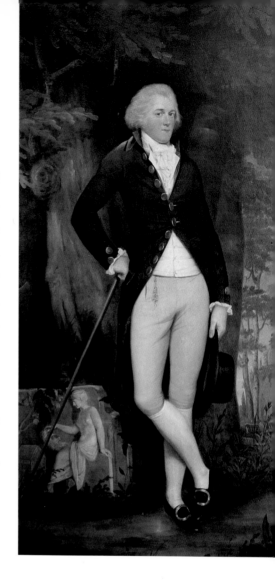

As Jane was the youngest but one of the family, her elder brothers were all preparing for their future careers while she was still in the nursery. James, ten years her senior, was the most studious of the boys, and obviously cut out to be a clergyman. He had benefited so much from his father's tuition in the classics as to be able to enter St John's College, Oxford, in the summer of 1779, at the remarkably early age of fourteen. Here he remained for the next ten years, coming home only for vacations, while studying first of all for his Bachelor of Arts degree, which he gained in 1783, and then staying on to become a Master of Arts in 1788, while holding a Fellowship at St John's. It seems that when Jane and Cassandra were with Mrs Cawley in Oxford James took them sightseeing round the colleges, through 'dismal chapels, dusty libraries and greasy halls', as Jane afterwards teased him.

Edward Austen (1767-1852), adopted by Mr and Mrs Knight in 1783. This portrait was probably painted in Rome, c.1789, during his Grand Tour of Europe, and shows the Temple of Minerva Medica in the background.

Jane Austen Memorial Trust.

The seeds of Edward Austen's future life were also planted in 1779, though at the time the eventual flowering could not have been foreseen. The Revd George Austen's wealthy Kentish cousin and benefactor Mr Thomas Broadnax May Knight was by now dead, and his son Thomas Knight II had inherited the estates of Steventon and Chawton in Hampshire, and of Godmersham, near Canterbury, in Kent, where he chose to live. Mr Thomas Knight II married in the spring of 1779 and brought his bride, Catherine Knatchbull, a member of a Kentish baronet family, to introduce her to his distant Austen cousins in Hampshire. Here they both took

a fancy to Edward Austen, then a sensible and attractive little chestnut-haired boy aged about 12; and when it became clear that they were fated to remain childless, they decided to adopt Edward and formally make him their heir. At first they asked only that Edward should come to spend his holidays with them, and Mr Austen was initially doubtful, fearing Edward would fall too far behind in his Latin studies. However, Mrs Austen, perhaps more worldly-wise, advised her husband to oblige his cousins and let Edward pay the visit as requested. This visit was obviously entirely satisfactory to the Knights and was followed by others, and the final outcome was that Edward's adoption was formally agreed upon in 1783. He stayed at home to be taught by his father until 1786, but instead of going to university was then sent abroad by the Knights on the Grand Tour, which lasted for four years. He visited

Thomas Knight II (1735-94) of Godmersham, and his wife Catherine Knatchbull (1753-1812), the wealthy cousins and patrons of the Austen family; by George Romney, 1781.

Private collection.

Germany and spent a year at Dresden University, went on to Rome, where he had his obligatory souvenir portrait painted, full-length with classical ruins and sculptural fragments in the background, and from there returned on a leisurely journey through northern Italy, Switzerland, western Germany and the Netherlands in the autumn of 1790. He then went to live permanently at Godmersham in order to learn how to manage a large estate and to prepare for his future place in Kentish society.

Henry too was originally destined for the church, and followed James to St John's College in 1788. While the brothers were together, James took advantage of Henry's assistance and started publishing a weekly journal called *The Loiterer* — an admiring imitation of Joseph Addison's *The Spectator* and Dr Johnson's *The Rambler*. It was originally planned to give 'a rough but not entirely inaccurate Sketch of the Characters, the Manners, and the Amusements at Oxford at the close of the eighteenth century' but later came to include a wider range of topical and amusing subjects. The essays and articles were mostly written by James and Henry themselves, with a few contributed by their undergraduate friends, and it ran for sixty issues until March 1790, when James finally left Oxford. The essays were all anonymous, but it is noticeable that in the ninth issue of the journal, 28 March 1789, a spoof letter to the editor appears, over the signature 'Sophia Sentiment',

Part of a page from James Austen's magazine The Loiterer, *showing the letter from 'Sophia Sentiment'.*

The British Library, P.P.6117.d.

THE LOITERER. 7

whatever you do, that your hero and heroine muſt poſſeſs a great deal of feeling, and have very pretty names. If you think fit to comply with this my injunction, you may expect to hear from me again, and perhaps I may even give you a little aſſiſtance;—but, if not—may your work be condemned to the paſtry-cook's ſhop, and may you always continue a bachelor, and be plagued with a maiden ſiſter to keep houſe for you.

Your's, as you behave,

SOPHIA SENTIMENT.

complaining about the lack of feminine interest and in particular the lack of romantic fiction in the issues to date: '... let us see some nice affecting stories, relating the misfortunes of two lovers, who died suddenly, just as they were going to church. Let the lover be killed in a duel, or lost at sea, or you may make him shoot himself, just as you please; and as for his mistress, she will of course go mad; or if you will, you may kill the lady, and let the lover run mad; only remember, whatever you do, that your hero and heroine must possess a great deal of feeling, and have very pretty names'. The tone of this burlesque letter is so much in keeping with Jane's own jokes and essays in her *Juvenilia* as to make it seem entirely likely that she also wrote this offering for her brother's magazine.

The next son, Francis, or Frank as he was usually known, was an active strong-minded little boy who enjoyed mathematics but not classical languages, and decided for himself that he wished to enter the Royal Navy. Neither the Austens nor the Leighs had any naval tradition or connections, but Mr Austen evidently saw no reason to try to thwart his son's wishes, and so entered him at the Royal Naval Academy in Portsmouth in April 1786, just before his twelfth birthday. Once a boy was accepted there his tuition was free, which may well have encouraged Mr Austen to agree to his son's choice of career. Frank completed his studies most satisfactorily, and left in 1788 with a glowing testimonial to the Lords of the Admiralty from the Academy's Governor, to be appointed as a Volunteer aboard HMS *Perseverance* for a year's practical training in seamanship under Captain Isaac Smith, after which he would be rated as a Midshipman. HMS *Perseverance* sailed for the East Indies in December 1788, and bearing in mind the dangers and hardships of naval life, the Steventon family must often have wondered if they would ever see Frank again. However, all went well with him; he became a Midshipman in 1789 as expected, removed from HMS *Perseverance* to HMS *Minerva* in 1791 and was promoted to Lieutenant in December 1792, while still aged only 18. He did not return to England from the East Indies until the end of 1793, and while he was away Jane wrote for him *The Adventures of Mr Harley* and *Jack and Alice*, as well as mentioning him in the same breath as Sir Francis Drake in her longer composition *The History of England:* 'Yet great as [Drake] was, and justly celebrated as a sailor, I cannot help foreseeing that he will be equalled in this or the next Century by one who tho' now

The Royal Naval Academy, Portsmouth. Both Francis and Charles Austen received their naval education here. The buildings still survive in Portsmouth Dockyard, but are no longer used as a Naval Academy and are not open to the public.

Lithograph by J.T. Lee, 1806; Portsmouth City Museum.

Opposite:

A Midshipman of 1799, drawn by Rowlandson. Francis and Charles Austen would have worn this uniform when starting their naval service.

but young, already promises to answer all the ardent and sanguine expectations of his Relations and Freinds, amongst whom I may class the amiable Lady to whom this work is dedicated [Cassandra], and my no less amiable self'.

As for Jane's own travels, her first recorded visit, apart from the brief schooling forays to Oxford, Southampton, and Reading, was to Kent in the summer of 1788, when her parents took her and Cassandra to Sevenoaks to call upon Mr

Austen's wealthy uncle and benefactor, Francis Austen, who had now reached the great age of 90 but was still capable of receiving and entertaining guests.   The Austens' Walter relations came to dine with them, but cousin Phylly, unlike Eliza de Feuillide, did not take to little Jane in the least, reporting that '[she] is very like her brother Henry, not at all pretty & very prim, unlike a girl of twelve ... Jane is whimsical and affected.'   On the return journey the Austens travelled via London to stay with Mrs Hancock and Eliza de Feuillide, who were then renting a house in Orchard Street but planning to return to France the following month.   This too is Jane's first recorded visit to London, and as soon as she got home London street names entered her *Juvenilia*; in *The Beautifull Cassandra* she teased her sister by associating her name with the cheerfully dishonest adventures of a milliner's daughter in Bond Street.

Charles, the youngest of the family — for whom Jane wrote *Sir William Mountague* and the *Memoirs of Mr Clifford* — followed in Frank's footsteps and entered the Royal Naval Academy in the summer of 1791, leaving in September 1794 and being appointed directly as a Midshipman aboard HMS *Daedalus*, whose commanding officer, Captain Thomas Williams, was by now the husband of the Austens' cousin Jane Cooper.   Charles did not sail to the East Indies, like Frank, but saw much service in home waters, which enabled him to pay flying visits to Steventon or to Edward in Kent whenever his ships returned to English ports for supplies or repairs.

Now that his sons were all out in the world Mr Austen could allow himself to wind down his tutorial work, and it seems that the last pupil probably left Steventon in or before 1795.   One of the bedrooms was then converted to a small family sitting-room, with bookshelves and Jane's piano, and these less-crowded living conditions undoubtedly enabled her to devote more and more of her time to writing.

Ashe rectory, as it is today. The house is no longer used as the rectory for the parish, and is in private ownership.

The Lefroy Family

By now Jane had found good friends in the neighbouring parish of Ashe, where the Revd George Lefroy, a married man with young children, had become rector in 1783. The Lefroys were of cosmopolitan outlook and considerably wealthier than the Austens, and proved a great asset to the neighbourhood, as they were very fond of society and most hospitable. Madam Lefroy, as she was usually referred to, was a very intelligent and well-read woman, charming and elegant, and although Jane Austen was

no doubt first invited to Ashe as a playmate for little Jemima-Lucy Lefroy, her own quick wits and literary interests soon made her a personal even if very youthful friend of Madam Lefroy herself. Jane in her turn admired her adult friend as a perfect model of gracefulness and goodness. The Lefroys were sufficiently well off not to need to take pupils, so Madam Lefroy busied herself by teaching the village children to read and write, as well as vaccinating all her husband's parishioners against smallpox, after Dr Edward Jenner's discovery of the benefits of vaccination had come to be generally accepted.

The Lefroys were also responsible for introducing other, more polished, newcomers into the rural Hampshire scene. Mr Lefroy's bachelor uncle Benjamin Langlois had been in the British Embassy in Vienna, and after returning to England had become a Member of Parliament and Under-Secretary of State; although he had his own house in London, he came to Ashe for the last few years of his life to join his nephew's family. He was remembered as 'a good and benevolent old man, with much diplomatic experience, but most fatiguingly ceremonious, with abilities not much above the common'; Jane perhaps used something of his character, years later, for Mr Woodhouse in *Emma*. Madam Lefroy's younger brother and sister, Egerton and Charlotte Brydges, came to Hampshire in 1786 in order to be near the Lefroys, and rented the vacant parsonage at Deane for two years from Mr Austen.   James Austen much admired Charlotte Brydges and wrote sonnets to her, and Egerton in turn proffered a versified epilogue for the Austens' production of *The Wonder* in 1787.

The Lefroys and Austens became linked by marriage in the next generation, when Jane's niece Anna married Madam Lefroy's youngest son, Benjamin, in 1814.

The Lloyd and Fowle families

In the spring of 1789 Mr Austen let Deane parsonage again, to a clergyman's widow, Mrs Lloyd, with her two daughters Martha and Mary.   The deceased Mr Lloyd had been the rector of Enborne, near Newbury in Berkshire, and the third daughter, Eliza, had recently married her cousin Fulwar-Craven Fowle of Kintbury, one of Mr Austen's former pupils, so there was already a chain of connection to bring the Lloyds into Hampshire.   Martha and Mary were both older than Cassandra and Jane, but they soon became firm friends and within a few months Jane wrote a flourishing dedication of *Frederic & Elfrida* to Martha 'as a small testimony of the gratitude I feel for your late generosity to me in finishing my muslin Cloak'.   The

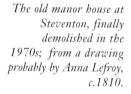

The old manor house at Steventon, finally demolished in the 1970s; from a drawing probably by Anna Lefroy, c.1810.

Jane Austen Memorial Trust.

Lloyd girls had a strange family story about their grandmother, 'the cruel Mrs. Craven', a scheming and probably adulterous gold-digger who had bullied and neglected her children; she had forced two of them into marriage, and another three daughters had taken the desperate and in those days unheard-of step of running away from home to take refuge with friends and marry wherever they could. Mrs Lloyd had had more success than her sisters in as much as she had met and married the Revd Nowys Lloyd, a respectable clergyman with a reasonable income from his parish of Enborne, although towards the end of his life he suffered from depression and became almost a recluse. Mrs Fowle, wife of the vicar of Kintbury, whose marriage had been arranged by her mother, was luckily quite content with her lot and happy with her family of four sons — Fulwar-Craven, Tom, William, and Charles — but the other Craven daughters had sunk into poverty and obscurity. To hear the saga of such an unhappy family life, so different from that of the supportive Austens and Leighs, must have made a great impression upon the young Jane, and was evidently the germ for the first of her serious adult works, the short novel-in-letters *Lady Susan*, probably composed in 1794. The Lloyds stayed at Deane until 1792 and then moved to Ibthorpe, a tiny village not far from Andover and about sixteen miles away from Steventon. The move did not sever the friendship with the Austens, and both Cassandra and Jane, and Martha and Mary, alternated in paying visits to each other and to the Kintbury family.

Hampshire Neighbours

Nearer home, the Digweed family had been tenants of Steventon manor-house itself and the 900-acre Manor Farm, owned by Mr Austen's Kentish cousins the Knights, for several generations. In Jane's time Mr and Mrs Hugh Digweed were the current occupants, and their four sons John, Harry, James and William were much of an age with the young Austens, and so must have been their earliest playmates. The Digweeds were prosperous and forward-looking agriculturalists, who were able to spend some £250 on constructing a large threshing-mill that was noteworthy in the neighbourhood, but their four sons do not seem to have shared any of the Austens' intellectual interests.

In the parish of Deane there were two estates, the larger of which had been owned for many generations by the Harwood family, who lived in the fine seventeenth-century red-brick Deane House adjacent to the church of All Saints. The current Squire, John Harwood VI, was a bucolic character who is reputed to have been the original of Squire Western in Fielding's *Tom Jones*, and not long after Mr Austen had come to Hampshire Mr Harwood was reported as saying: 'You know all about these sort of things. Do tell us. Is Paris in France, or France in Paris? for my wife has been disputing with me about it'. There were three Harwood sons, again much of an age with the Austens, but, as with the Digweeds, no match for them in intellect. John VII was worthy and conscientious but dull, Earle was boastful and quarrelsome and a constant worry to his family, while the youngest, Charles, was in Jane's view simply 'thick-headed'.

The other estate in Deane was that of Oakley, where young Mr Wither Bramston had recently rebuilt his manor-house of Oakley Hall following his marriage to Mary Chute, a daughter of yet another landowning family. A cousin of Mr Bramston recorded sourly in his diary that the latter was 'little better than a blockhead', and certainly his unmarried sister Augusta was considered very eccentric by the neighbourhood and cordially disliked in consequence. The Bramstons were childless, but Mrs Bramston was 'civil, kind and noisy' and always willing to be helpful and friendly. Her family, the Chutes, lived in a much larger Tudor mansion at Sherborne St John near Basingstoke, where her elder brother William neglected the estate in his passion for fox-hunting; he did, however, appoint James Austen as vicar of Sherborne St John in 1791.

In the parish of Ashe, apart from the Lefroys at the rectory, the only other gentleman of note was Mr Holder of Ashe Park, a wealthy but uninteresting middle-aged bachelor who lived off the proceeds of his West Indian plantations. He was given to making 'infamous puns', but was hospitable and obliging in his heavy way, and Jane could at least appreciate the comforts he was able to provide for guests at Ashe Park.

The last of the families within easy visiting distance of the Austens were the Terrys at Dummer with their thirteen children, some of whom eventually married into these other local gentry circles. Although Jane in her later life said there was

Manydown, Hampshire. Home of the Bigg-Wither family for many generations, and where Jane might have lived had she married Harris Bigg-Wither following his proposal in 1802. The house was demolished in 1960.

nothing like the situation of three or four families in a country village to make a good setting for a novel, it seems unfortunate that none of the Steventon and Deane neighbours could offer sons suitable to provide successful love-stories for herself and her sister.

All these families, with others of higher rank, looked towards Basingstoke as the nearest town for shopping and socialising, as well as for long-distance travel, as it lay on the stagecoach routes from London which divided there, one going through Winchester to the south-west of England, and the other going through Overton and Andover to Bath and further west. Every winter, public assembly balls were held monthly in the big room at the Town Hall in Basingstoke market place, and it would be feasible for families from roughly a ten-mile radius to attend a ball and return the same night, unless they were able to arrange to stay with friends and return the next morning. Alternatively, those with sufficiently large houses could give private dances at home for a select few, as the Lefroys did at Ashe Rectory, or the Bigg-Withers at Manydown Park, near Basingstoke. This latter family had come to live at Manydown in 1789 upon inheriting the estate from a distant cousin, and after Martha and Mary Lloyd left Deane the three unmarried daughters Elizabeth, Kitty and Alethea, became in their turn the close friends of Jane and Cassandra. They had just one younger brother, Harris Bigg-Wither, a tall, rather sickly boy with a bad stammer, whom his anxious father did not dare send away to school.

The old Town Hall and Assembly Rooms (demolished in the 1830s) in Basingstoke market place. Jane danced here at the monthly balls held during the winter, and wrote of similar scenes when creating the Bennet girls in Pride and Prejudice

Willis Museum, Basingstoke.

New family circles

The first of Jane's brothers to get married was, not surprisingly, Edward. Following his return to Godmersham at the end of 1790, he soon fell in love with Elizabeth, an eighteen-year-old brown-haired beauty, one of the thirteen children of the neighbouring baronet, Sir Brook Bridges of Goodnestone. They were married in the spring of 1791 and started their married life at Rowling, a small manor-house provided for them by the Bridges, where their first four children were born. Their eldest daughter, Fanny, when she reached her teens, became Jane's favourite niece, and Jane described her as 'almost another sister'. Fanny's diaries, which she kept meticulously from childhood onwards, were not noticed by any of Jane's biographers before 1989; however, now that they have been studied it can be seen that they provide a number of references to her aunt, and so fill in many hitherto missing dates in Jane's life.

James was ordained in June 1789, and finally left Oxford in the spring of 1790 to become curate of Overton, the nearest little town to Steventon. Here he met General Edward Mathew and his wife Lady Jane, daughter of the Duke of Ancaster; the General had recently returned from the West Indies and was renting the old manor-house at nearby Laverstoke. The Mathews had three daughters, of whom the second, Anne, had turned thirty but was still single. She was pale, tall and elegant and unusually slender, with beautiful large dark eyes and 'a good deal of nose', but by the standards of the day was practically middle-aged. The Mathews did not consider the young curate to be a very good match for a Duke's grand-daughter, but James had always had a weakness for elegant aristocratic young women, and Anne must have seen in him her last chance of matrimony. Eventually therefore the General gave his consent and provided Anne with an allowance of £100 a year to add to James's income of £200; they were married in the spring of 1792 and came to live at Deane parsonage after the Lloyds had moved to Ibthorpe. Their only child, Anna, was born in April 1793, and her memories, recorded years later, are a further source of information about Jane Austen's life.

Elizabeth Bridges (1773-1808), wife of Edward Austen Knight. Miniature by unknown artist, c. 1790.

Jane Austen Memorial Trust.

However, James's happiness was only short-lived, for Anne Mathew — perhaps too pale and slender to be healthy — died suddenly in the spring of 1795, and little Anna had to live with her grandparents at Steventon Rectory while James recovered from his bereavement. It was obviously sensible that he should marry again, and in January 1797 he chose a more practical helpmate and brought back to Deane parsonage the family's old friend Mary Lloyd. Poor Mary was neither elegant nor beautiful, as her face was badly scarred

Silhouette of Mary Lloyd (1771-1843), second wife of James Austen; probably made by her son James Edward Austen-Leigh, c.1825.

Private collection.

as a result of smallpox in childhood, but she was a devoted wife and mother and made James very happy. They had two children, James Edward and Caroline; many years later James Edward Austen-Leigh (as he had then become) wrote the first biography of his aunt, *A Memoir of Jane Austen*, to which both Anna and Caroline contributed their memories.

Cassandra seemed to have an assured future before her, as she became engaged in the winter of 1792-93 to Revd Tom Fowle, the second son of the Kintbury family, and one of her father's old pupils. At the moment, Tom was the rector of the very small parish of Allington near Amesbury in Wiltshire, but this did not provide an income sufficient to support a wife and family. His kinsman the Earl of Craven had promised him one or other of the more valuable Shropshire parishes that were in his gift, whenever one should fall vacant, so Cassandra had to be content to wait till such time as Tom could provide a home for her in Shropshire.

Out in the World

As for Jane herself, she 'came out' into society in the autumn of 1792, not long before her 17th birthday, and the opinion of the neighbourhood was that though not an absolute beauty, she was nevertheless a very pretty girl. She was tall and slender and a good dancer, with fine naturally curling chestnut brown hair and bright hazel eyes; her face was rather round than long, with a clear brown complexion and a bright but not a pink colour, and a small but well-shaped nose. A one-time resident of Ashe, Mrs Mitford, a plain dumpy woman and mother of an equally plain, fat little girl, saw Jane at about this time, probably at one of the Basingstoke assembly balls, and in later years jealously described her as 'the prettiest, silliest, most affected, husband-hunting butterfly she ever remembered'. The earliest of Jane's own letters that survive date to January 1796, and certainly from her light-hearted comments to Cassandra it would appear that at the age of 20 there were several young men in Hampshire and Berkshire who were ready to admire her: 'Tell Mary that I make over Mr Heartley & all his Estate to her for her sole use and Benefit in future, & not only him, but all my other Admirers into the bargain wherever she can find them, even the kiss which C. Powlett wanted to give me, as I mean to confine myself in future to Mr Tom Lefroy, for whom I donot care sixpence. Assure her also as a last & indubitable proof of Warren's indifference to me, that he actually drew that Gentleman's picture for me, & delivered it to me without a Sigh'.   Mrs Austen herself seems to have been aware that her younger daughter's talents were such as would make it difficult to find a husband to suit her; when James announced his engagement to Mary Lloyd, Mrs Austen wrote the latter a kind motherly letter of welcome, adding: 'I look forwards to you as a real comfort to me in my old age, when Cassandra is gone into Shropshire, & Jane — the Lord knows where'.

Tom Lefroy

Of the various young men to whom Jane refers at this time, the only friendship which might perhaps have blossomed into romance was in fact that with Tom Lefroy.   Tom was one of the Irish nephews of the Lefroys of Ashe, a fair, good-looking, serious and scholarly young man, very slightly younger than Jane Austen, and destined by his family for the Bar.   In the autumn of 1795 he had just completed his degree at Trinity College, Dublin, and came to visit his English uncle and aunt for a Christmas holiday.   He and Jane danced and flirted together at four balls during December and January, to such an extent that, although the Austens do not seem to have disapproved of the idea, the Lefroys became alarmed that the flirtation might lead to a formal engagement between the very youthful and penniless couple.   Madam Lefroy in particular thought that Tom was to blame for paying court to Jane when he knew he was in no financial position to support a wife, and so saw to it that he was sent off to London to continue his legal studies at Lincoln's Inn under the watchful eye of his great-uncle Benjamin Langlois.   So far as is known, Tom and Jane never met again, and although Jane had declared to Cassandra that she would not mind at all when he left Ashe, it does seem that, for the moment at least, she had become fonder of him than she cared to admit.   Madam Lefroy preferred not to mention his name to the Austens until a safe period of time had elapsed, so it was not until November 1798 that Jane had any further news of him: '... I was too proud to make any enquiries; but on my father's afterwards asking where he was, I learnt that he was gone back to London in his way to Ireland, where he is called to the Bar and means to practise'.   Tom did become a very successful barrister and lived to a great age, ending his career as the Lord Chief Justice of Ireland, solemn and deeply religious, and the owner of a fine estate in County Longford. He married a Dublin friend's sister in 1799, but although his marriage was very happy, he never forgot Jane Austen, and to the last year of his life remembered her as the object of his youthful admiration, as he admitted to a nephew decades later.

Further Afield

Jane was now old enough to pay independent visits to Edward and Elizabeth and their rapidly increasing young family at Rowling, and so stepped into a completely new circle of acquaintances amongst the Kentish landed gentry, in the area from Faversham and Ashford eastwards to Canterbury and the coastal towns of Ramsgate, Margate, Dover and Deal. Her first trip seems to have been in the summer of 1794, and it was probably on this occasion that she met and for a few days 'fondly doted' upon

young Mr Edward Taylor of Bifrons, for the sake of his 'beautiful dark eyes', as she joked to Cassandra a couple of years later. Thanks to his wife Elizabeth and her numerous brothers and sisters, all of whom in due course married into local landowning families, Edward's social connections spread throughout this eastern corner of Kent, and during her visits to him Jane was able to take her place within this network and so meet people who were on the whole more wealthy and sophisticated than those in Hampshire. Jane noticed the difference, as she wrote in amusement to Cassandra: 'Kent is the only place for happiness, Everybody is rich there ... let me shake off vulgar cares & conform to the happy Indifference of East Kent wealth ...' The lifestyle enjoyed by Edward became even more comfortable and prosperous when he moved from Rowling to Godmersham in 1797, soon after the death of his adoptive father Mr Thomas Knight II — the 'Elegance & Ease & Luxury' of Godmersham, as Jane appreciatively commented. Mrs Knight, with dowager propriety, settled herself in a large town house in Canterbury, which made a most useful reason for shopping expeditions to the city that could include a call upon her as well. Although Mrs Knight's affections were centred upon Edward ('From the time that my partiality for you induced Mr Knight to treat you as our adopted child I have felt for you the tenderness of a Mother'), she was also unfailingly 'gentle & kind & friendly' to his sisters, as Jane commented gratefully to Cassandra after one such visit. When the family's benefactress died in October 1812, Edward formally changed his surname, much to the annoyance of his daughter Fanny, who wrote in her diary: 'Papa changed his name about this time in compliance with the will of the late Mr Knight and we are therefore all *Knights* instead of dear old *Austens* — How I hate it!!!!!!'

Travelling westward from Hampshire rather than eastward, Jane also had her first taste of social life in Bath, thanks to her uncle and aunt Mr and Mrs Leigh-Perrot. They had purchased there No 1 Paragon Buildings, a tall narrow town house standing high upon the cliff edge overlooking the river Avon, and in November 1797 Mrs Austen and her daughters stayed with the Leigh-Perrots for some weeks. It is probable that Jane and Cassandra had passed through Bath in the summer of 1794, when they went to Gloucestershire to stay with Leigh relations, but this visit in the winter of 1797 is the first time Jane is definitely known to have been in the city which figures so prominently in two of her novels. As the Leigh-Perrots were town-dwellers, middle-aged and childless, their social interests were rather more staid and circumscribed than those of Edward's Kentish landowner friends, and it may be that Jane's unhappiness at the idea of living in Bath (as recorded by family tradition) stemmed from the restrictions and artificiality imposed by the conventions of a wealthy urban lifestyle.

However, her next visit, in the summer of 1799, was certainly more enjoyable, for on this occasion Edward and Elizabeth and their two eldest children came for a six-week holiday, and brought Jane and Mrs Austen with them as their guests. Edward rented No 13 Queen Square to accommodate his party, and immediately upon arrival Jane wrote to Cassandra, staying at home in Steventon with their father: 'We are exceedingly pleased with the House; the rooms are quite as large as we expected, Mrs Bromley [the landlady] is a fat woman in mourning, & a little black kitten runs about the Staircase'. Her succeeding letters talk of exploring the neighbourhood — 'We took a very charming walk from 6 to 8 up Beacon Hill, & across some fields to the Village of Charlcombe, which is sweetly situated in a little green Valley, as a Village with such a name ought to be' — attending the 'grand gala on tuesday evening in Sydney Gardens; - a Concert, with Illuminations & fireworks', going to the theatre, and undertaking shopping commissions for the other members of the family; she was, however, quite satisfied with the length of the holiday and looking forward to her return home.

Revolution and War

While English life continued peacefully enough under the Hanoverian rule of George III and the established Church of England, across the Channel the great divide between the miseries of the French peasantry and the extravagances of the court at Versailles broke apart in 1789 into open revolution. The English government, rightly wary of an unstable political situation in a nation traditionally the enemy of England, in December 1792 called up the local county-based militia regiments, to defend the country in the event of invasion. The militia were not part of the standing army and were not obliged to serve abroad, but by their presence at home released the regular troops for warfare overseas. During the summer they

were encamped at various strategic points on the coastline, and once the bad weather of winter had set in, which would make it difficult if not impossible for an invasion to take place, the men were quartered wherever accommodation could be found for them in nearby towns and villages.

After vain attempts to reach some compromise between the opposing interests of the Revolution, Louis XVI and his family were dethroned and imprisoned. In 1793 the King was guillotined on 21 January and on 1 February the new republic of France declared war on Great Britain and Holland — a war that lasted until 1815 and whose campaigns stretched across the globe. The course of Henry Austen's life now changed, for although he had taken his degree at Oxford and in a few months' time could have proceeded to ordination, he preferred to 'offer his services in the general defence of the Country' — as he wrote in later years — and in April 1793 became a Lieutenant in the Oxfordshire Militia.   For the next six years he and his regiment moved round the southern and eastern counties of England, and they also spent a year in Dublin when it seemed likely that the French might invade via Ireland.   In 1798, when French troops were massed along the Channel coast, squires and clergy of English parishes were instructed to plan for the defence and if need be evacuation of their villages; Steventon's report was that there were 29 able-bodied men, but armed only with their agricultural tools, to protect 78 non-combatants, and the local transport and supplies — most of which belonged to the Digweeds and the Austens — amounted to 34 draft- and four riding-horses, 12 waggons and five carts, 1100 sheep and 64 pigs, and the crops of hay, wheat, oats and barley.

For Jane's brothers Frank and Charles, who were already in the Navy anyway, the outbreak of war meant for them opportunities for promotion and prize-money (a share in the value of the ships and cargoes captured in naval warfare), and they miraculously survived healthy and unharmed during all their years of active service. Frank fought mainly in the Mediterranean and the Baltic, and Charles, after serving

Opposite:
A French corvette, prize to the ship in the offing, *watercolour by Lieut F. O. Skinner, 1804.*
In pre-photographic days, naval and military officers received drawing lessons, as part of their training, to enable them to sketch harbours and fortifications, etc. Hence in Mansfield Park *Fanny cherishes 'a small sketch of a ship sent four years ago from the Mediterranean by William, with H.M.S. Antwerp at the bottom, in letters as tall as the mainmast'.*

The British Library, Add.MS.33642, f. 74.

Women and children gathering heath. *Revd John Skinner drew this group of cottagers near Basingstoke, as he rode from Hampshire into Berkshire in 1821. Some of Mr Austen's parishioners may have looked like this.*

The British Library, Add.MS. 33658, f. 121.

several years in home waters, was sent out to the West Indies and spent some time in Bermuda. For many months at a stretch they were out of touch with the family at home in Steventon, and Jane's letters often refer to hurried notes or messages sent by her brothers via other naval officers who had received orders to return to England.

As Jane's cousin Eliza was married to a Frenchman, it is not surprising that she was the member of the family who suffered most at this period. While the Comte de Feuillide was busy with works of land reclamation on his estate in the south of France, Eliza and her mother had been accustomed to travel back to England from time to time to keep in touch with the Austens and the Walters. In 1791 Mrs Hancock had fallen ill while in London, and died in the spring of 1792; the Comte was able to visit England to comfort Eliza, but soon had to return to France at the command of the Revolutionary Government, under pain of having his property confiscated. It seems that Eliza loyally but unwisely followed him back to France some months later, perhaps hoping that the revolutionary fervour would not infect their tenants at Nérac. However, the Comte's peasantry resented his enclosure of their one-time common marshlands, and started to sabotage the reclamation works and to attack his employees when rents were claimed. Eliza and her husband were in Paris early in 1794, perhaps planning then to flee to England, but in the event Eliza escaped alone. The Comte was arrested in Paris, tried on a trumped-up charge, and guillotined the same day, 22 February 1794. It is not known whether he himself had ever visited the Austens in Hampshire, but with both mother and husband dead Eliza must have sought comfort from her uncle, and probably stayed at Steventon in the spring of 1794, bringing first-hand news of the horrors then being enacted in France directly into the peaceful English parsonage.

Cassandra too had her life changed by the outbreak of war, for in 1795 the French threatened the English possessions in the West Indies, and an expeditionary force was sent out to protect the islands. Tom Fowle's kinsman and patron, the young Earl of Craven, had recently become colonel of The Buffs, the 3rd Regiment of Foot, and his troops formed part of the force under the command of General Abercromby which sailed out during the winter of 1795-96. Lord Craven asked Tom to accompany him as his private chaplain, and Tom, not wishing to offend his patron by refusing on the grounds of his engagement to Cassandra, went with him in January 1796. He survived for a year, but then like so many of the English troops, succumbed to yellow fever and was buried at sea off St. Domingo; by a cruel irony, he was expected to return home in May 1797, but instead the news came that he had died the previous February. Lord Craven was reported to have said afterwards that had he known of Tom's engagement he would never have allowed him to go to so dangerous a climate. Cassandra did not become in any way reclusive or melancholic as a result of this tragic ending to her hopes, but evidently never found anyone else to replace Tom in her affections, and so as the years went by devoted herself to being a good daughter, sister and aunt within the immediate Austen family circle.

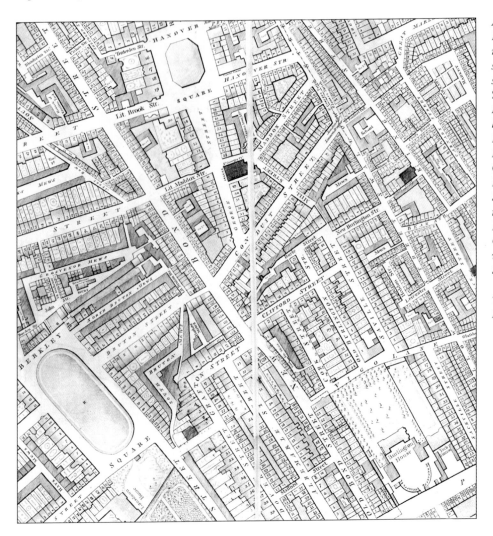

A section of Richard Horwood's map of London, 1799, showing some of the streets mentioned in Sense and Sensibility; *Mrs Jennings has a handsome house in Berkeley Street, Lady Middleton is in Conduit Street, the Palmers in Hanover Square, Willoughby takes lodgings in Old Bond Street, and Gray's the jeweller's was at No. 41 Sackville Street.*

The British Library, Map Library

Jane's first three novels

As Jane had spent so much of her childhood in literary composition, it is not surprising that she continued this pastime in her adult days, and so began to write full-scale mature novels, though still only for the amusement of her family and without thought of publication.   Into these novels she was now able to put the knowledge of places and events which she had gained in recent years; for example, in 1795 she wrote *Elinor and Marianne*, the prototype for *Sense and Sensibility*, which is set partly in London and partly in Devon.   The London streets and shops

Mr George Austen's letter of 1st November 1797, offering to send the manuscript of First Impressions *to the London publisher Cadell.*

St John's College, Oxford, MS.279.

mentioned are those Jane would have seen for herself when visiting Eliza de Feuillide, and the imaginary village of Barton, some four miles north of Exeter, probably owes its existence to the fact that the South Devon Militia were quartered in Hampshire during the winters of 1793-94 and 1794-95, some of their companies actually located in Basingstoke.   Here Jane would have met and danced with the young officers at the monthly assemblies, and heard a great deal about the Exeter neighbourhood from them, as they all came from that area.   From her brother Henry, too, whose service with the Oxfordshires had taken him around the south coast of England, she would have heard tales of the social and moral problems that inevitably arose when large contingents of rootless young men, of all ranks of society, suddenly descended upon a hitherto peaceful country town.   It was indeed these problems which led the War Office to undertake a crash programme of barrack-building from 1792 onwards, until by 1797 nearly a hundred barracks had been constructed capable of housing some 70,000 men, and the old practice of quartering troops upon the civilian population ceased to exist.

Bath Assembly Rooms; aquatint engraving by Thomas Rowlandson from his set of drawings entitled The Comforts of Bath, *1798.*

Victoria Art Gallery, Bath.

In 1796 Jane wrote *First Impressions*, the prototype for *Pride and Prejudice*, in which the plot hinges largely upon the arrival of a militia regiment in Hertfordshire. Jane obviously could not give a genuine name to the regiment in which she placed the deceitful Wickham, and so referred to them merely as 'the ——shires', but it was in fact the Derbyshire Militia that was quartered in Hertford and Ware during the winter of 1794-95. As Mr Austen had an elderly clerical cousin in Welwyn, near Hertford, no doubt the Steventon family heard from him of the arrival of these North Country strangers in his district, thus inspiring Jane to create Mr Darcy and his estate of Pemberley in Derbyshire. Jane's images of Lady Catherine de Bourgh's Rosings Park and Mr Collins's parsonage at Hunsford in Kent were probably created from her memories of houses and estates in the vicinity of Godmersham.

The Austen family enjoyed *First Impressions* so much that Mr Austen himself considered it worthy of publication, and in November 1797 he wrote to the well-known London publisher Thomas Cadell, offering to send the manuscript for his consideration. Unfortunately, Mr Austen did not refer in any way to the wit and comedy of his daughter's text, so it was perhaps not surprising that his letter was endorsed by Cadell's clerk: 'declined by Return of Post'. As Jane herself was very modest in her own assessment of her work, she had probably never expected that her manuscript would be accepted and so, luckily, was not discouraged by this initial rebuff; she returned instead to improving *Elinor and Marianne* and re-titling it *Sense and Sensibility*.

Jane's third novel, *Northanger Abbey*, was written during 1798-99, and memories of her visit to the Leigh-Perrots in Bath in 1797 provided the necessary information to set Catherine Morland's entry into the social scene there. Quite probably Jane and her aunt had been pushed and squeezed in the crowded Assembly Rooms just as Catherine and Mrs Allen were: 'With more care for the safety of her new gown than for the comfort of her protégée, Mrs Allen made her way through the throng of men by the door, as swiftly as the necessary caution would allow; Catherine, however, kept close at her side, and linked her arm too firmly within her friend's to be torn asunder by any common effort of a struggling assembly' — and all the other details of the geography of the city and surrounding countryside are entirely accurate. Catherine's happy childhood at the imaginary Fullerton parsonage — 'rolling down the green slope at the back of the house...cricket, baseball, riding on horseback, and running about the country' — sounds remarkably like Jane's own life at Steventon, in a household that included five brothers and Mr Austen's pupils as well; while the 'horrid' novels which Catherine enjoys reading and by which her imagination is led astray, are all genuine best-sellers of the period and those which Jane and her family read together. This story was originally called simply *Susan* — the heroine's name was not changed to Catherine until some years later, and the title of *Northanger Abbey* was in fact given to it by Henry Austen after Jane's death.

Mrs Leigh Perrot (1744-1836); engraving made at the time of her trial. 'Mrs Leigh-Perrot appeared very pale and emaciated, between fifty and sixty years of age, and rather thin. She was dressed in a very light lead-colour pelisse, a muslin handkerchief on her neck, with a cambric cravat. Her hair of a dark-brown, curled on her forehead; a small black bonnet, round which was a purple ribband, and over it a black lace veil, which was thrown up over her head.'

The Lady's Magazine, April 1800.

Grand Larceny

One family event that was not reflected in any of Jane's writings was the totally unexpected near-calamity which befell her aunt, Mrs Leigh-Perrot. She and her husband had by now settled into a routine of spending half the year in their Berkshire home of Scarlets, and the other half at No 1 Paragon in Bath, and were well-known in the city as a rich and highly respectable elderly couple. On 7 June 1799 Mrs Leigh-Perrot had called at a haberdasher's shop to enquire as to their stock of lace; and it seems that the managers of the shop — who had just then taken over from bankrupt owners and were themselves of doubtful reputation — decided to blackmail this worthy lady when next she came in. As it happened, Mrs Leigh-Perrot returned the very next day and bought some black lace to trim a cloak, but some white lace was also deliberately included in her small parcel. When she and her husband passed the shop again half an hour later, the manageress, Miss Gregory, ran out and demanded to examine her parcel, finding of course the white lace within it. Miss Gregory and her lover Charles Filby, whom she officially employed as a shop-assistant, then went to the Bath magistrates and laid a charge against Mrs Leigh-Perrot of stealing lace to the value of twenty shillings (£1.00 in modern decimal currency), as well as sending an anonymous note to Mrs Leigh-Perrot threatening her with exposure.

As the value of the lace was more than one shilling (£0.05), the crime of which Mrs Leigh-Perrot was accused was that of grand larceny, which could carry a death sentence; in practice, however, a reprieve could result in the alternative of transportation to Botany Bay in Australia for a term of fourteen years. The Bath magistrates had no alternative but to commit Mrs Leigh-Perrot for trial in March of the following year, and in the meantime the couple were remanded to lodge in the gaol-keeper's house. The gaol-keeper and his wife were not unpleasant people, and did their best to treat their unwilling guests kindly; but their small house in the centre of the prison buildings was cramped, dirty, smelly and noisy, and the Leigh-Perrots had to endure these squalid conditions for some six months before their case came to be tried. In the meantime they received other anonymous letters from Bath, warning them that this was a blackmail plot and that Miss Gregory and her friends expected to be bought off before the trial commenced.

THE

TRIAL

OF.

JANE LEIGH PERROT,

WIFE OF

JAMES LEIGH PERROT, Efq;

CHARGED WITH

STEALING a CARD of LACE,

IN THE SHOP OF

ELIZABETH GREGORY,

HABERDASHER and MILLINER, at BATH,

BEFORE

Sir SOULDEN LAWRENCE, Knight,

ONE OF THE JUSTICES OF HIS MAJESTY'S COURT OF KING'S BENCH.

AT TAUNTON ASSIZES,

On Saturday the 29th Day of March, 1800.

TAKEN IN COURT BY

JOHN PINCHARD, Attorney,

Of TAUNTON.

TAUNTON:

Printed by and for THOMAS NORRIS, White-lion-court;
And Sold by CARPENTER and Co. 14, Old Bond-ftreet; E. NEWBERY,
St. Paul's Churchyard; HURST and Co. Paternofter-Row, London;
MEYLER, Bath; SHEPPARD, Briftol; COLLINS, Salifbury;
NORRIS, and POOLE, Taunton; and all other Bookfellers,

*Title-page of
The Trial of
Jane Leigh-Perrot,
a pamphlet published
in Taunton at the time.*

It says much for Mrs Leigh-Perrot's strength of character that she refused to yield to the blackmailers despite the extreme discomfort she and her husband were enduring.   The Austens did their best to support her, as she wrote to others: 'My dear Affectionate Sister Austen, tho' in a state of health not equal to *trials* of any kind, has been with the greatest difficulty kept from me.   In a letter from her a few days ago I had the pain to hear of her Valuable Son *James* having had his Horse fall with him by which his leg was broken.   This is a loss indeed because he had been a perfect Son to me in Affection and his firm Friendship all through this trying Business had taught me to look to him and his Wife (a Relation of Lord Craven's well bred and sensible) to have come to us at the Assizes [session of the court].   *Now* I can neither ask Mother or Wife to leave him nor could I accept the Offer of my Nieces — to have two Young Creatures gazed at in a public Court would cut one to the very heart'.

The trial took place at Taunton on 29 March 1800, and lasted some seven hours, during which Miss Gregory and her associates produced a now well-rehearsed tale, claiming actually to have seen Mrs Leigh-Perrot pick up the card of white lace from a box on the counter.   The criminal law, as it then stood, made it very difficult for Mrs Leigh-Perrot to prove her innocence;   she was not allowed to give evidence on oath on her own behalf, her husband was not allowed to give evidence for her, and her counsel were not allowed to address the jury on her behalf but could only examine and cross-examine witnesses.   However, her lawyers were able to cast doubts on the accusers' characters and honesty, other witnesses testified to having had extra items included amongst their purchases, and numerous respectable friends of the Leigh-Perrots testified to her high moral standards.   The judge's summing-up lasted nearly an hour, and it took no longer than fifteen minutes for the jury to bring in a verdict of Not Guilty.

The couple returned to Bath immediately, and Mrs Leigh-Perrot wrote of her reception there: '... before *10* on Monday Morning our anxious Friends began coming in ... my whole time has been taken up in *kissing* and Crying ... To be sure (as a kind Friend told me) I stand some chance of being killed by Popularity — tho' I have escaped from *Villainy* ...That these wretches had marked me for somebody timid enough to be scared and *Rich* enough to pay handsomely rather than go through the terrible Proceedings of a public Trial nobody doubts ...'   Mrs Austen invited the couple to come to Steventon to recuperate, so they were probably there during the summer of 1800. Literary critics sometimes claim that Jane Austen knew nothing of the uglier side of life, which is why her novels deal only with matchmaking amongst the gentry and professional classes of society; but this sudden calamity occurring in her own family circle proves them wrong

Last years at Steventon

Another visitor to Steventon in the summer of 1800 was Henry Austen, whose regiment moved from Dorset to the Isle of Wight at this time. During his militia career Henry had been promoted to captain and regimental paymaster, and now that the immediate emergency of a possible invasion had subsided, he was planning to resign from the Oxfordshires and set himself up in London as a banker and army agent. He had the more reason for wishing to settle into civilian life, as he had married his widowed cousin Eliza de Feuillide at the very end of 1797 and so was stepfather to her little boy Hastings, who unfortunately had grown up in some way physically or mentally handicapped and was by now a complete invalid. Although Henry was ten years her junior their marriage nevertheless proved very happy. The Austens may have been initially surprised at the match, but were obviously quite in approval, as Mr Austen sent a present of £40 to the regiment to pay for the wedding-party celebrations. Henry resigned in January 1801, and set himself up with an office and home in suitably smart districts of London.

The sole inhabitants of Steventon parsonage were now therefore Mr and Mrs Austen, both elderly and not in the best of health, while their daughters were well into their twenties and still unmarried. It may have been the Leigh-Perrots who persuaded Mr Austen that he and his wife would feel better if they retired to Bath, and that Jane and Cassandra would stand more chance of finding husbands in a larger social circle. Whatever reasons or discussions there may have been, the final decision was obviously very sudden. In November 1800 Cassandra was visiting Edward at Godmersham, and Jane was with the Lloyds at Ibthorpe; she returned from there accompanied by Martha Lloyd, and family tradition records that as they entered the rectory hall Mrs Austen greeted them with: 'Well, girls, it is all settled, we have decided to leave Steventon in such a week and go to Bath'. The news was such a shock to Jane that she was 'greatly distressed' and is said to have fainted.

✒ *Bath and the West Country*

'All vapour, shadow, smoke & confusion'

Family tradition recalled that Jane loved the country, and her delight in natural scenery was such that she would sometimes say she thought it must form one of the joys of heaven.   It may well have been the prospect of exchanging her childhood home and the woodlands and fields of Hampshire for a tall narrow terrace house in one of Bath's hot stone-paved streets which upset her so much; but as a young single woman with no income of her own she had no choice but to remain with her parents and abide by their decisions.   She therefore put a brave face on it, and wrote to Cassandra: 'I get more & more reconciled to the idea of our removal. We have lived long enough in this Neighbourhood, the Basingstoke Balls are certainly on the decline, there is something interesting in the bustle of going away, & the prospect of spending future summers by the Sea or in Wales is very delightful. — For a time we shall now possess many of the advantages which I have often thought of with Envy in the wives of Sailors or Soldiers' — adding with her usual irony: 'It must not be generally known however that I am not sacrificing a great deal

Queen Square, Bath, 1819. In 1799 Jane and her family stayed for some weeks at No 13, on the south side of Queen Square.

in quitting the Country — or I can expect to inspire no tenderness, no interest in those we leave behind'.

The bustle of going away continued throughout the spring of 1801; it was agreed that James should become his father's curate and move into Steventon rectory. From some comments in her letters it seems that Jane suspected Mary Lloyd had been the instigator of Mr Austen's sudden decision to retire, and was both surprised and rather hurt at the eagerness James and his wife displayed in cuckooing their parents out of their old home. In May the family moved to Bath, staying with the Leigh-Perrots for the time being while house-hunting — they were united in disliking Axford Buildings, Cassandra wanted to avoid Trim Street, Mrs Austen liked the idea of Queen Square and Mr Austen preferred Laura Place. Jane hoped for either Charles Street, as it was close to Kingsmead Fields, or else somewhere near Sydney Gardens, and she was the one who had her wish gratified, as a three-year lease of No 4 Sydney Place was found to be available. While the landlord redecorated the premises the family went off on one of the seaside holidays Jane had been anticipating, and did not return to Bath until October to superintend the fitting up of their new home.

Only one letter of Jane's survives from the period May 1801 to January 1805, that of 14 September 1804, written from Lyme Regis during another summer holiday. Much of her life at this period has therefore to be reconstructed from the memories of other members of the family, recorded in later years. James and Mary visited Bath in April 1802, bringing nine-year-old Anna with them. She was very fond of her grandparents and was delighted to see how much they were enjoying their retirement and the cheerfulness of city life, and how her tall white-haired grandfather was still so handsome as to attract everyone's notice when he appeared in public. Although Anna was too young to realise it, Bath's social life was in fact now on the decline, as the younger and more fashionable people were following the Prince of Wales to his favourite resort of Brighton on the South Coast. Bath was instead becoming the home of retired army and naval officers, seeking a mild climate in

Above:

Sydney Place, Bath. No. 4 Sydney Place, where the Austens lived from 1801-04.

Left:

Sidmouth Bathing Place. *Watercolour by Revd John Skinner, 1797.*

The British Library, Add.MS33635, f. 66.

which to recover from the fevers and wounds gained on active service, or of elderly people, such as Mr and Mrs Austen, who had enjoyed the city in its heyday. The Assembly Rooms were no longer crowded out, because an ageing population preferred to hold small private parties at home. Mr and Mrs Leigh-Perrot were themselves a case in point — he now suffered from gout, she had a bad bronchial cough and was growing deaf — and Jane's letters in 1801 speak resignedly of her aunt's dull little card-parties which she was obliged to attend.

West Country holidays

The first seaside trip, during the summer of 1801, seems to have been to the South Devon coast — Sidmouth and Colyton, where one of Mr Austen's old pupils, Revd Richard Buller, was the vicar. In 1802 the first phase of the war with France came to a temporary end, when the Peace of Amiens was in force from March 1802 to May 1803; with the resultant demobilisation of soldiers and sailors Charles Austen was able to join his family in Bath and from there they went that summer to Dawlish and Teignmouth (also on the South Devon coast), with possibly a Welsh journey as well encompassing Tenby and Barmouth. At some time in 1803 the Austens were at Ramsgate in Kent, and they may also have gone to Charmouth, Up Lyme and Pinny, on the Dorset coast; certainly they visited Lyme Regis in Dorset, whether or not for the first time, in the November of that year, and evidently liked it so much that they returned for a longer visit in the summer of 1804. On this second trip they were accompanied by Henry and Eliza, and at Lyme the party divided, Jane staying with her parents and Cassandra continuing on to Weymouth with the others — hence Jane's letter to her of 14 September. This was the last of the seaside holidays, as Mr Austen died the following January, and without his income as rector of Steventon his family could no longer afford such luxuries. Jane used her memories of these trips to good effect when she wrote *Persuasion* years later.

Failed Romances

If the Austens had hoped that Jane and Cassandra might find husbands in Bath society, they were disappointed, and further disappointments were in store. At the end of the summer in 1802, Charles Austen escorted his sisters over to Godmersham, and after some weeks there they returned to Bath via Steventon. Here they also stayed some weeks, and in the course of this visit went for a few days to their friends the Bigg-Withers at Manydown. On the evening of 2 December Harris Bigg-Wither, now 21 but still plain, awkward and stammering, proposed to Jane, and she accepted him; the next morning, however, she withdrew her consent, and both she and Cassandra returned at once to Steventon and insisted that James should escort them back to Bath immediately.

No letters of Jane's survive from this period, and her reasons for acting as she did can only be guessed at; but it would seem that her long friendship with Harris's elder sisters (who had perhaps prompted him to make this proposal), and the obvious worldly advantages she would gain by becoming mistress of a fine house and estate, had temporarily swayed her judgement. She was by now 27 and well aware that once her father died his dependants would have only a very small income, but overnight consideration evidently made her realise she could not accept the man himself, however desirable such a match might otherwise be.

There is also the family tradition that on one of these West Country holidays between 1801-04 Jane did meet a man whom she could have loved and who was, in Cassandra's opinion, suitable in every way. No contemporary evidence or information is available, because it was not until some twenty years later, long after Jane was dead, that Cassandra mentioned the matter to her niece Caroline. One of James-Edward Austen's friends, a charming and good-looking young man named Henry Edridge, died very suddenly, and the shock of this sad news evidently startled Cassandra into remembering a similar situation, and telling her long-kept secret: that one summer by the sea the Austens had met someone rather like Henry Edridge — a gentleman 'unusually gifted with all that was agreeable', who was 'greatly attracted' by Jane during the holiday friendship, and 'was urgent to know where they would be the next summer, implying or perhaps saying that he should be there also, wherever it might be ... Soon afterwards they heard of his death'. Cassandra was firmly of the impression that he had fallen in love with her sister and was quite in earnest, and she did not doubt, either, that he would have been a successful suitor. In the absence of any further evidence, however, Jane's stillborn romance can only remain nameless and dateless.

Literary work

The move to Bath and subsequent journeyings meant Jane had less time to concentrate on creative writing, and during this period there is a break in what previously had been a steady literary output. She had, however, kept her manuscripts by her, and now, with the family's encouragement and using Henry's lawyer Mr Seymour as her agent, she succeeded in selling *Susan (Northanger Abbey)* to the London publisher Richard Crosby in 1803, for £10, with a stipulation for early publication. Crosby even advertised the work as being in the press, but then changed his mind and never brought it out. In the meantime Jane started another full-length novel, probably in 1804, of which she completed in fact only the first few chapters; possibly she grew discouraged when she eventually realised that *Susan* was not going to appear after all. The fragment is known as *The Watsons*, though this may not be the title Jane herself would have given it.

Last years in Bath

When the Austens returned from the seaside at the end of October 1804 the lease on No 4 Sydney Place had expired, and instead they rented No 3 Green Park Buildings, rather nearer the centre of Bath but facing the Kingsmead fields and with a fine view of Beechen Cliff across the river Avon which looped round the lower end of Kingsmead. Only two months later they received the sad news from Steventon that Madam Lefroy of Ashe had been killed in a road accident not far from her home, on 16 December — by a cruel irony, Jane's own 29th birthday. Jane's immediate reaction to the news is not known, but four years afterwards she wrote some verses in memory of the dear friend of her girlhood, still grieving at her loss and remembering her virtues and kindnesses. And within another month, bereavement happened at home, when her father died peacefully on 21 January 1805, after only two days' sudden illness. He was buried at Walcot church a few days later, and Mrs Austen and her daughters now had to come to terms with their altered circumstances, both social and financial. In those days ladies did not travel far from home without the protection of a male companion, so that in future Mrs Austen would have to rely upon the availability and goodwill of her sons to escort herself and her daughters upon any journeys they wished to make. Furthermore, there were no

Opposite:

Broad Street, Lyme Regis, in the 1830s. '... *the principal street, almost hurrying into the water* ...' - Persuasion.

Philpot Museum, Lyme Regis.

To the Memory of Mrs Lefroy,
who died Dec:r 16. — my Birthday. — written 1808.

The day returns again, my natal day;
What mix'd emotions with the Thought arise!
Beloved friend, four years have pass'd away
Since thou wert snatch'd forever from our eyes.

The day, commemorative of my birth
Bestowing Life & Light & Hope on me,
Brings back the hour which was thy last on Earth.
Oh! bitter pang of torturing Memory!

Angelic Woman! past my power to praise,
In Language meet, thy Talents, Temper, Mind,
Thy solid Worth, thy captivating Grace!
Thou friend & ornament of Humankind!

At Johnson's Death, by Hamilton t'was said,
"Seek we a substitute — Ah! vain the plan,
No second best remains to Johnson dead —
None can remind us even of the Man."

So we of thee — unequall'd in thy race.
Unequall'd thou, as he the First of Men.
Vainly we search around thy vacant place,
We ne'er may look upon thy like again.

Come then fond Fancy, thou indulgent Power —
— Hope is despending, chill, severe to thee! —
Bless thou, this little portion of an hour,
Let me behold her as she used to be.

Memorial verses to Madam Lefroy, written by Jane on 16 December 1808.

Winchester Cathedral Library

Opposite:

The uniform of a Post Captain, by Rowlandson, 1799. Both Frank and Charles Austen would have worn this uniform as they gained promotion.

pensions for the clergy, so the income from Steventon would now all go to James, succeeding his father as rector of the parish. Here again, Mrs Austen was now largely dependent upon her sons' ability and goodwill to contribute towards the upkeep of herself and her daughters, as her own income was very small. Unlike the miserly John Dashwood of *Sense and Sensibility*, the Austen sons did all they could in their respective ways to look after their mother and sisters, and Mrs Austen exclaimed gratefully that never were children so good as hers. It was decided that in future Mrs Austen should divide her time between visiting her sons in the summer and retiring to rented accommodation in Bath during the winter

For the next year Jane's life was restless and unsettled, as these family visits took place one by one. After giving up the lease of No 3 Green Park Buildings at the end of the March quarter, the Austen ladies lodged for a few months at No 25 Gay Street before travelling to Godmersham via Steventon. From Godmersham they went on to Worthing, in Sussex, for an autumn seaside holiday, and here they were joined by their old friend Martha Lloyd, the elder sister of James's wife Mary. The widowed Mrs Lloyd had died in the previous spring, and it seems Martha preferred to join forces with Mrs Austen and her daughters rather than become her sister's pensioner at Steventon. The Austens returned to Bath, again via Steventon, in the spring of 1806, and Mrs Austen took lodgings in Trim Street while looking round for some house or apartments to rent on a more permanent basis.

It was now Frank Austen who provided a longer-term solution for his mother's accommodation. He had been made Post-Captain in 1800 — a rank which ensured a good salary and continuing promotion within the Navy — and with this firm financial standing and prize money in addition, he was able to get married in the summer of 1806 to a Ramsgate girl named Mary Gibson, whom he had met in 1803 when on naval duties in Kent. It was Frank's idea that, as his young wife was bound to be lonely when he was away at sea, it would be sensible if she lived with Mrs Austen and her daughters, and so it was arranged that they would all — Martha Lloyd included — move to Southampton and rent a house there, which would be conveniently close to the great naval dockyard of Portsmouth.

Trip to the Midlands

On 2 July 1806 Mrs Austen and her daughters left Bath for the last time — 'with what happy feelings of Escape!' Jane recalled, two years later — and set off, via Clifton, on a trip to Gloucestershire to stay with one of Mrs Austen's cousins, Revd Thomas Leigh of Adlestrop rectory. Mr Leigh, who was a rich, gentle old bachelor living with his spinster sister Elizabeth, had called in the great landscape gardener Humphrey Repton in 1802 to improve the Adlestrop property by making a new garden for the rectory which merged with the parklands of his nephew's bigger Adlestrop House nearby. Repton charged a fee of five guineas a day (£5.25) for his services, as Mr Leigh evidently informed his cousins when showing them round his improvements — a fee which can be compared with the fact that a country curate might have an income of no more than one guinea (£1.05) a week upon which to live and possibly keep a family.

The Austens did not stay long at Adlestrop, for an unusual chain of family circumstances sent Mr Leigh and his guests scurrying off to another family property, that of Stoneleigh Abbey in Warwickshire. This large estate had been owned by distant cousins of the Adlestrop Leighs, and the last Lord Leigh had left an oddly-worded will that failed to make clear who was to inherit the property after his last surviving sister's death. Upon her death on 2 July, the Revd Thomas Leigh's lawyers advised him to take possession as fast as he could and so forestall other possible claimants. Stoneleigh Abbey, as its name implies, had once been a monastery but

*The west front of
Stoneleigh Abbey,
Warwickshire.
Revd Thomas Leigh
became the owner of
this mansion in 1806.
'There are 45 windows
in front, (which is
quite strait with a flat
Roof) 15 in a row ...'*

Jarrold Publications

had passed into the hands of the Leigh family in 1561, who then built a new house using the stones of the old abbey and some of its foundations. Early in the eighteenth century the third Lord Leigh had remodelled the west wing into a new principal front, though leaving the remainder of the Elizabethan house unaltered, and the whole formed a rich and handsome estate.

Mr Leigh's party arrived early in August, and Mrs Austen wrote delightedly to Mary Lloyd a few days later: 'And here we all found ourselves on Tuesday ... Eating Fish, venison & all manner of good things, at a late hour, in a Noble large Parlour hung round with family Pictures — every thing is very Grand & very fine & very Large — The House is larger than I could have supposed — we can *now* find our way about it, I mean the best part, as to the offices (which were the old Abby) Mr Leigh almost dispairs of ever finding his way about them — I have proposed his setting up *directing Posts* at the Angles — I expected to find everything about the place very fine & all that, but I had no idea of its being so beautiful, I had figured to myself long Avenues, dark rookeries & dismal Yew Trees, but here are no such melancholy things ... I will now give you some idea of the inside of this vast house, first premising that there are 45 windows in front, (which is quite strait with a flat Roof) 15 in a row —

you go up a considerable flight of steps (some offices are under the house) into a large Hall, on the right hand, the dining parlour, within that the Breakfast room, where we generally sit, and reason good, tis the only room (except the Chapel) that looks towards the River, — on the left hand the Hall is the best drawing room, within that a smaller, these rooms are rather gloomy, Brown wainscoat & dark Crimson furniture, so we never use them but to walk thro' them to the old picture Gallery; Behind the smaller drawing Room is the State Bed chamber with a high dark crimson Velvet Bed, an *alarming* apartment just fit for an Heroine, the old Gallery opens into it — behind the Hall & Parlour a passage all across the house containing 3 staircases & two small back Parlours — there are 26 Bed Chambers in the new part of the house, & a great many (some very good ones) in the Old ...' Although Mrs Austen herself was obviously visiting Stoneleigh for the first time, it may be that Jane and Cassandra had already seen it in 1794 when they first travelled into Gloucestershire, for the house does seem to bear a considerable resemblance to the fictitious Northanger Abbey.

The day after Mrs Austen wrote her letter, she and her daughters went on northwards to the village of Hamstall Ridware, just over the border into Staffordshire, where her nephew Revd Edward Cooper had been the rector since 1799, rearing his large family in comfort and making a name for himself in clerical circles by publishing a number of his sermons. Edward Cooper was plump and jovial enough, but not one of Jane's favourite relations — it seems she found him pompous and too enthusiastically pious in the Evangelical style. The Austens stayed with the Coopers for about five weeks, and from there returned to Steventon and so on to Southampton, where they arrived early in October 1806.

~ *Southampton*

Castle Square

The Austens took lodgings in Southampton – the exact address of which is unknown – while they looked around for a house to rent. Jane presently fell ill with whooping-cough, and her first few months in this new town were definitely unhappy. Cassandra went to spend Christmas at Godmersham, and Martha Lloyd went to Kintbury, so in their stead James and Mary came from Steventon bringing their toddler Caroline with them. The brunt of the arrangements for entertaining fell upon Jane's shoulders, and her letters to Cassandra in January 1807 sound weary and downcast: 'When you receive this, our guests will be all gone or going; and I shall be left to the comfortable disposal of my time, to ease of mind from the torments of rice puddings and apple dumplings, and probably to regret that I did not take more

Southampton: the High Street in the early nineteenth century, looking northwards towards the Bath Gate. This was one of the original entrances through the stone walls of the medieval city. The classical building to the right of the Bar Gate is All Saints church, where Jane and her family worshipped. It was destroyed by bombs in 1940.

pains to please them all'. The weather was in general too bad for exercise, and James, who hated to be confined indoors, was bored and restless, while Mary Lloyd apparently made no attempt to conceal her lack of interest in the books which Jane had chosen for the family's usual evening pastime of reading aloud. Frank's wife Mary Gibson was already pregnant and feeling unwell in consequence; and the Southampton gentry who came to call appeared to Jane to be irritatingly wealthy: 'They live in a handsome style and are rich, and she seemed to like to be rich, and we gave her to understand that we were far from being so; she will soon feel therefore that we are not worth her acquaintance'. It seems as if Jane was suddenly very depressed by the limitations of the life now imposed upon the family, reduced as they were to a small group of an elderly widow and two spinster daughters.

As the year advanced, however, matters improved, for Frank took the lease of 'a commodious old-fashioned house in a corner of Castle Square ... [it] had a pleasant garden, bounded on one side by the old city walls; the top of this wall was sufficiently wide to afford a pleasant walk, with an extensive view, easily accessible to ladies by steps.' This section of the city walls, though today surrounded by reclaimed land used for industrial purposes, was in Jane's time washed by the tides of Southampton Water, with the wooded slopes of the Isle of Wight visible across the estuary. The centre of Castle Square itself was then occupied by 'a fantastic edifice, too large for the space in which it stood, though too small to accord well with its castellated style, erected by the second Marquis of Lansdowne'. This strange house stood on the partly demolished foundations of the keep of the medieval Southampton Castle, and the rather eccentric Marquis had rebuilt it into his idea of what an ancient castle ought to have looked like.

Helping her mother plan a new layout for the garden cheered Jane up, as well as the constructive work of supervising the cleaning and furnishing of the house, and the family moved in early in March 1807. 'We hear that we are envied our House by many people, & that the Garden is the best in the Town –' she wrote to Cassandra. Frank almost immediately received his next naval appointment – the command of HMS *St Albans*, then at Sheerness in Kent, for convoy duty to and from South Africa, China and the East Indies – and so was absent from Southampton when his first daughter, Mary-Jane, was born on 27 April. He did however manage to have

another month of home life before setting sail for the Cape of Good Hope on 30 June. It was probably during these spring months that Frank took Jane over to Portsmouth, as she later remembered in *Mansfield Park*: 'The day was uncommonly lovely. It was really March; but it was April in its mild air, brisk soft wind, and bright sun, occasionally clouded for a minute; and every thing looked so beautiful under the influence of such a sky, the effects of the shadows pursuing each other, on the ships at Spithead and the island beyond, with the ever-varying hues of the sea now at high water, dancing in its glee and dashing against the ramparts with so fine a sound ...'

As Southampton was much closer to London, Steventon and Godmersham than Bath had been, it was now easier for the Austen sons to keep in touch with their mother. In April Edward came from Kent to inspect his other estate at Chawton, recently vacated by its latest tenant, and came again in June to say goodbye to Frank.

Watercolour of the beach at Portsmouth, c.1808, with naval ships in the background.

Portsmouth City Art Gallery

Plans were then made for a family gathering, so Edward brought Elizabeth and the elder children to Chawton Great House in August, Mrs Austen and her daughters joined them there, and James brought his family over from Steventon. When the Austen ladies returned to Southampton in mid-September, Edward and his family in turn followed them, and his daughter Fanny's diary records several days of cheerful family pleasures – going to the theatre, taking a trip by water to Hythe, strolling in Southampton High Street in the summer evenings – and Henry rushed down from London to organise a picnic amidst the romantic ruins of Netley Abbey. As the months passed the Austens did find some congenial acquaintance amongst the Southampton neighbours, so the year of 1807 ended much more happily for Jane than it had begun.

Family Journeyings

Now that Martha Lloyd was living with the Austens permanently, almost as a third daughter, it was easier for Jane and Cassandra to travel together to visit their friends or brothers, secure in the knowledge that Mrs Austen would be happy at home in Martha's company. This is unfortunate for biographers, in as much as there are obviously no letters from Jane to Cassandra at such periods – of which the spring of 1808 is one. From other sources it can be learnt that during January and February the sisters were together paying visits in Hampshire and Berkshire, first of all to Steventon and then to Kintbury. While at Steventon they visited Manydown; it is not known whether Harris Bigg-Wither was there at the time, but Jane's refusal of his proposal had in no way affected her friendship with his sisters and she maintained contact with them to the end of her life.

At Kintbury they stayed at the vicarage with their old friends the Revd Fulwar-Craven Fowle and his family. One of his sons, another Tom, was already in the Navy, serving as a Midshipman under Charles Austen's command in Bermuda; but his eldest son, Fulwar-William, was at home during this visit by the Austen sisters, and many years later recorded his memories of Jane at this time: '… she was pretty – certainly pretty – bright & a good deal of color in her face – like a doll – no that wd. not give at all the idea for she had so much expression – she was like a child – quite a child very lively & full of humor – most amiable – most beloved –'

Jane's next trip was to London in May to stay with Henry and Eliza for a month, and from there she went on to Godmersham with James and Mary Lloyd, for another month. Edward and Elizabeth now had ten children and Elizabeth was pregnant again; Jane thought she did not look very well, and so relieved her of some of her maternal duties by helping to teach the younger children their lessons. Frank returned home from the East Indies in July, and his next task was to take soldiers out to Portugal to participate in the Peninsular War – another phase of the long-drawn-out struggle against Napoleon. As HMS *St Albans* stood off in Mondego Bay, Frank could see the first British victory of the campaign, the battle of Vimeiro, in progress on the clifftop. He returned to Southampton with the wounded troops and French prisoners, and while waiting for his next orders, took lodgings for himself and Mary Gibson and their baby Mary-Jane in Yarmouth on the Isle of Wight. Fond as he was of his mother and sisters, Frank obviously felt he would prefer more privacy for himself and his wife than the Castle Square house could afford, and Jane commented: '... with fish almost for nothing, & plenty of Engagements and plenty of each other, [they] must be very happy'.

Bereavement at Godmersham

Elizabeth Austen's eleventh baby was due at the end of September, and Cassandra went to Godmersham to help look after the family and household while the confinement took place. Edward's sixth son, Brook-John, was born safely on 28 September and Elizabeth seemed to be making a normal recovery, but a fortnight later she suddenly collapsed and died within half-an-hour. Jane's letters to Cassandra of 13 and 15 October were full of love and sympathy for the bereaved household: 'We have felt, we do feel, for you all – as you will not need to be told – for you, for Fanny, for Henry, for Lady Bridges, & for dearest Edward, whose loss and whose sufferings seem to make those of every other person nothing ... We need not enter into a Panegyric on the Departed – but it is sweet to think of her great worth – of her solid principles, her true devotion, her excellence in every relation of Life ...' Edward's two eldest sons, now teenage schoolboys at Winchester College, came for some days compassionate leave at Southampton, and Jane did her best to cheer and comfort them with walks and river trips during the day and parlour games in the evenings.

Leaving Southampton

Cassandra naturally stayed on at Godmersham for several months, helping Fanny, barely sixteen, to begin shouldering the responsibilities so suddenly thrust upon her – mistress of a large household, surrogate mother to ten brothers and sisters, and companion to her grieving father. Some of Jane's letters at this time seem to be missing, but it is evident that this bereavement made Edward wish to keep in closer touch with his mother and sisters, and he made Mrs Austen the offer of a house on one of his estates – either at Wye, near Godmersham, or at Chawton, near the Great House there. As Henry had now opened a branch of his London bank in the Hampshire town of Alton, Mrs Austen had already been considering moving there, particularly in view of the fact that rents in Southampton were rising rapidly – and as Chawton was hardly more than a mile from Alton, this was her obvious preference. Edward therefore earmarked for them a large cottage at the crossroads on the edge of the village, which until recently had been occupied by his steward for the Chawton estate. Jane wrote to Cassandra: 'Everybody is very much concerned at our going away, & everybody is acquainted with Chawton & speaks of it as a remarkably pretty village; & everybody knows the house we describe – but nobody fixes on the right'.

Another attempt at publication

It was agreed that the Austen ladies should stay at Godmersham while the Chawton house was being refurbished for their occupation, and just before they left Southampton in April 1809 Jane made a sudden despairing attempt to secure the publication of her long-forgotten manuscript of *Susan*. She wrote to Crosby & Co., using the assumed name of 'Mrs. Ashton Dennis', offering to supply them with a second copy of the manuscript if they had lost the one sold to them in 1803, and suggesting she would publish it elsewhere if they were no longer interested. This letter did prod Mr. Crosby into action, but only to write curtly by return of post that '... there was not any time stipulated for its publication, neither are we bound to publish it, Should you or anyone else we shall take proceedings to stop the sale. The MS shall be yours for the same as we paid for it.' As £10 would have been a large amount for Jane to find out of her tiny income, she had to let the matter rest.

Jane's draft copy of her letter of 5 April 1809 to the publisher Richard Crosby, reminding him of her manuscript of Susan.

The British Library, Add.MS.41,253.B, f. 12

Gentlemen

In the spring of the year 1803 a M.S. Novel in 2 vol. entitled Susan was sold to you by a Gentleman of the name of Seymour, & the purchase money £10. rec.d at the same time. Six years have since passed, & this work of which I am myself the Authoress, has never to the best of my knowledge, appeared in print, tho' an early publication was stipulated for at the time of Sale. I can only account for such an extraordinary circumstance by supposing the M.S. by some carelessness to have been lost; & if that was the case, am willing to supply You with another Copy if you are disposed to avail yourselves of it, & will engage for no farther delay when it comes into your hands. — It will not be in my power from particular circumstances to command this Copy before the Month of August, but then, if you accept my proposal, you may depend on receiving it. Be so good as to send me a Line in answer, as soon as possible, as my stay in this place will not exceed a few days. Should no notice be taken of this address, I shall feel myself at liberty to secure the publication of my work, by applying elsewhere. I am Gentlemen &c &c

M. A. D.

Direct to Mrs Ashton Dennis
Post office, Southampton

April 5.
1809.

~ *Chawton*

'*Our Chawton home*'

The village of Chawton is in north-east Hampshire, about fifty miles from London. One of the main coach roads passed through both Alton and Chawton, dividing just outside the Austens' new home – the right fork went to Winchester and Southampton, and the left to Fareham and Gosport – and a wide shallow pond lay at the junction of the roads. Mrs Austen and her daughters arrived there from Godmersham on 7 July 1809, and this was Jane's last home until her death eight years later. The Cottage (as it came to be called by the family) had been built in the seventeenth century as an inn, and was an L-shaped red-brick two-storeyed building with a tiled roof, containing six small bedrooms as well as garrets above for storage or servants' rooms; the rectory at Steventon (demolished in 1824) was probably very similar, and no doubt Mrs Austen felt all the more comfortable at living in a house which reminded her of her married home. There were enclosed grounds behind the Cottage which included domestic outbuildings set round a small courtyard, a shrubbery walk, lawns, orchard, a kitchen garden where Mrs Austen happily planted her own vegetables and soft fruits, and flower-beds that were Cassandra's province. Cassandra also shared the housekeeping with Martha Lloyd, leaving Mrs Austen free for her daytime gardening and evening knitting and patchwork. Edward provided his mother with a donkey-cart – the period equivalent of a very small car – so that she could drive into Alton for shopping.

About five minutes' walk from the Cottage down the Gosport road lay Chawton Great House, set on a wooded slope above the rather decrepit little church of St Nicholas. The mansion was a rambling building, the old original part facing the road being flint and stone, while at the rear two red-brick gabled wings had been tacked on during the middle of the seventeenth century, necessitating extra staircases and awkward passageways. The current tenant was a widower, Mr John Middleton, who had six young children, and a sister-in-law, Miss Maria Beckford, for his hostess. Across the road from the church and Great House was the new rectory, built by the present incumbent, the Revd John Papillon, in 1803. When Mrs Knight heard that the Austens were moving to Chawton, and that the rector was a bachelor, she hoped he might prove a very suitable husband for Jane; to which kind thought Jane cheerfully responded to Cassandra: 'I am very much obliged to Mrs Knight for such

Chawton Great House, seen from across the meadows.

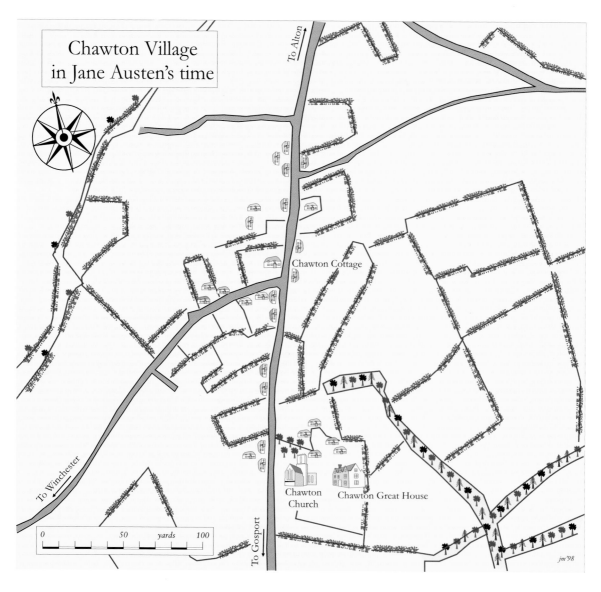

Chawton Village
in Jane Austen's time

To Alton

To Winchester

Chawton Cottage

Chawton
Church

Chawton Great House

To Gosport

0   50   yards   100

jm'98

Chawton village in Jane Austen's time. The Cottage stood at the junction of the main coach-roads from Winchester and Gosport to London.

Re-drawn from eighteenth-century estate maps belonging to the Knight family, and now in Hampshire County Record Office.

a proof of the interest she takes in me – & she may depend upon it, that I *will* marry Mr Papillon, whatever may be his reluctance or my own. – I owe her much more than such a trifling sacrifice.'

Other respectable neighbours in the village were Mr William Prowting, magistrate and Deputy Lieutenant for Hampshire, with his two daughters Catherine-Ann and Ann-Mary, both rather younger than the Austen sisters. At Chawton Lodge, close to the Cottage, lived Mr and Miss Hinton, children of the previous rector of Chawton; and, renting a leaky tumbledown cottage owned by one

The drawing-room and dining-parlour of Chawton Cottage as they are today.

Jane Austen Memorial Trust

of the villagers, the unfortunate Miss Benn eked out a frugal existence. She was the middle-aged spinster sister of the Revd John Benn, rector of the adjacent parish of Faringdon, and as Mr Benn had a dozen children to rear, he could not support her in addition. Miss Benn's situation was an uncomfortable reminder to Jane and Cassandra that, but for their own brothers' support, such a life might have been their fate as well.

A little further afield, in Alton, lived Mr and Mrs Harry Digweed – one of the sons of the Steventon family who had married Jane Terry from the Dummer family, so these old friends were frequent callers at Chawton. Mrs Digweed was not clever but very good-natured, and Jane was quite fond of her: 'Dear Mrs Digweed! – I cannot bear that she shd. not be foolishly happy after a Ball'. Henry's branch bank, Austen Gray & Vincent, was at No 10 Alton High Street, and letters could now be exchanged with him by enclosing them in the bank's correspondence parcels to and from the head office in London, Austen Maunde & Tilson; he would also of course be able to visit his family whenever he came down from London on business. In addition, Frank's wife Mary Gibson had moved to Alton, ahead of Mrs Austen, and was living at Rose Cottage, expecting her second child, while Frank was absent for probably two years on his next long voyage to China. As Steventon itself was less than twenty miles away, James and his family were able to call quite often, and Anna in particular, now an impetuous and emotional teenager who did not get on very well with her stepmother Mary Lloyd, was delighted to come and stay for weeks at a time with her grandmother and aunts as a relief from home. When Mr Middleton gave up his tenancy of the Great House in 1813, Edward did not re-let it but began to use it as a holiday home for himself and his children, as well as lending it to Frank for the same purpose. In 1811 Charles returned from Bermuda with his wife Fanny Palmer and the two little girls, Cassy and Harriet, who had been born to them out there. He and his family stayed from time to time in Chawton, either at the Cottage or the Great House, so Mrs Austen had the pleasure of seeing her family circle practically re-created around her.

Successful publication

At long last Jane was in a peaceful and congenial environment again, and almost as soon as the family had unpacked, she read through her *Juvenilia* volumes and could not resist making one or two little updating alterations here and there. It seems that it was now quite accepted by the rest of the family that her particular interest and hobby was literary composition. Although one of her domestic tasks was to prepare the family's breakfast at nine o'clock in the morning, and also to keep a tally on the stores of wine, tea and sugar (these latter two were then very expensive luxuries), there is no suggestion that she was in any way scolded or harassed for spending her spare time writing, which might have been the case if her relations had been less sympathetic. Her daily life was very quiet and regular; practising some simple songs and country-dances on her pianoforte in the morning, sewing and embroidering clothes, walking to Alton for shopping trips or strolling in the fine beechwoods of the Great House estate, playing with the ever-increasing numbers of nephews and nieces who called or stayed at the Cottage as the years went by – and now, above all, writing.

It is unfortunate that Jane and Cassandra were apparently not separated between July 1809 and April 1811, for in the absence of any letters it cannot be precisely known when Jane was persuaded by her family to try once again to get a manuscript published. This time, probably in the autumn of 1810, she submitted *Sense and Sensibility* to Thomas Egerton of Whitehall; and this time, the manuscript was accepted for publication upon commission (that is, at the author's expense), even though Jane was so sure 'its sale would not repay the expense of publication, that she actually made a reserve from her very moderate income to meet the expected loss'. At the end of March 1811 Jane went to London to stay with Henry and Eliza in their smart new house in Sloane Street and attended the large musical evening party they gave on 23 April. She was able to correct some proof-sheets of the first few chapters while she was there. Henry was a most enthusiastic agent and assistant, urging Egerton's printers on his sister's behalf, and publication was promised for May; however, for some unknown reason the book did not in fact appear until the end of October 1811. At that period it was considered rather improper for respectable ladies to write for money and general publication, so the title-page merely showed it as being 'By A Lady'. The work received some quite favourable reviews, and the first edition was sold out by July 1813, leaving Jane with a clear profit of about £140 after payment of expenses. The money was undoubtedly a very welcome addition to her small finances, but still more important was the favourable reception of the novel. Had it been a failure she would hardly have dared to make a second venture, so, on the success of *Sense and Sensibility* hung the existence of *Pride and Prejudice*.

It seems that once *Sense and Sensibility* was actually going through the press in Egerton's hands in the spring of 1811, Jane returned to *First Impressions* for a final check and revision with a view to offering it for publication if she could afford to do so. She herself said that she 'lop't and crop't' the text, and the action as it now stands fits the calendar of 1811-12 rather than that of 1796-97, but it is impossible to guess precisely what alterations and contractions she may have made. The title had to be changed, as another novel called *First Impressions* had been published in London in 1800, and Jane came across the neat phrase 'Pride and Prejudice' in *Cecilia*, a novel by her favourite authoress Fanny Burney – which also had the advantage of matching very well with *Sense and Sensibility*. At some time in the autumn of 1812 Jane submitted the manuscript to Egerton, and on this occasion he had no hesitation but bought the copyright from her for £110. Nor was there any delay this time in publication, for it appeared at the end of January 1813, and proved so popular that a second edition was necessary in the autumn of that year. The title-page read: 'By the Author of "Sense and Sensibility"', and the literate public were puzzled and intrigued as to the identity of the writer. One gentleman 'celebrated for his literary

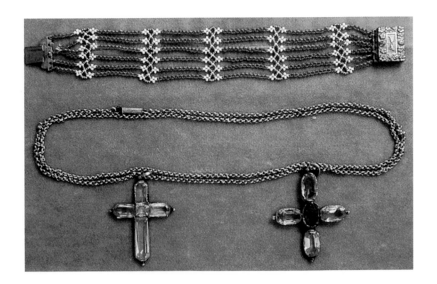

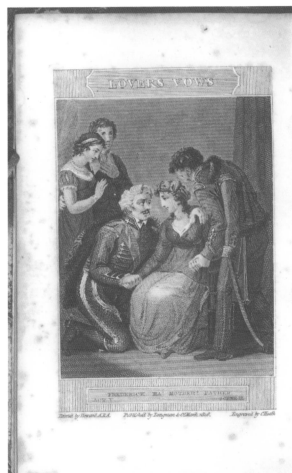

LOVERS VOWS

FREDERICK. HA! MOTHER! FATHER!
ACT V. SCENE.

Drawn by Howard, A.R.A. *Publd. Augt. by Longman & Co March. 1808.* *Engraved by C. Heath.*

LOVERS' VOWS;

A PLAY.

IN FIVE ACTS;

ALTERED FROM THE GERMAN OF KOTZEBUE,

BY MRS. INCHBALD.

AS PERFORMED AT THE

THEATRE ROYAL, COVENT-GARDEN.

PRINTED UNDER THE AUTHORITY OF THE MANAGERS

FROM THE PROMPT BOOK.

LONDON:

PRINTED FOR LONGMAN, HURST, REES, ORME, AND BROWN.
PATERNOSTER-ROW.

attainments' all unknowingly advised Henry Austen himself to read it, adding: 'I should like to know who is the author, for it is much too clever to have been written by a woman'. The witty playwright Richard Brinsley Sheridan told a friend to 'buy it immediately for it was one of the cleverest things he ever read'.

Mansfield Park

By the New Year of 1813 Jane was already half-way through *Mansfield Park*, the first of her mature novels to be written and published straight off, without any revisions or delays. Fanny Price is too quiet and shy to suit the taste of many modern readers, but perhaps the Austen family challenged Jane to create a heroine who would be the exact opposite to Elizabeth Bennet and yet succeed in finding her own appropriate love-match too. Much of the background in this work can be traced either to Jane's own experiences or else to information provided by other members of the family. Mansfield Park itself is probably based on Godmersham, mentally re-located near Northampton – in the spring of 1813 Jane, who had never been there, was writing round to enquire 'whether Northamptonshire is a country of Hedgerows'. Her knowledge of Portsmouth, gained while living in nearby Southampton, provides the detail for Fanny's miserable visit to her parents' shabby home off the High Street, and the accuracy of Mr Price's naval gossip comes from listening to Frank and his friends at this same period – she also used the names of some of the ships Frank had served on, punctiliously asking his permission to do so. The episode of Fanny being given an amber cross by her midshipman brother William is a clear reflection of Charles Austen giving his sisters a topaz cross each, bought with his prize money in 1801. Repton's charge of five guineas a day, quoted for improvements at the fictional Sotherton, is the actual figure paid by the Revd Mr Leigh at Adlestrop; while Jane's memories of the amateur theatricals years ago at Steventon were the inspiration for showing how a pastime innocent enough in itself can lead to the calamities caused in the Bertram family if an improper play is chosen and too enthusiastically performed. Jane probably finished her text in the autumn of 1813, and the book was published, again by Egerton, in May 1814. It sold steadily, despite the fact that it was never reviewed, and by the autumn of 1814 the first edition was exhausted, bringing Jane a profit of £350. It was perhaps this lack of reviewing which caused Jane to keep a list ('Opinions of Mansfield Park') of the comments she received from her family and the few people in the neighbourhood who now knew the secret of her authorship; the eccentric Miss Augusta Bramston of Oakley Hall 'owned that she thought S.&S.- and P.& P. downright nonsense, but expected to like MP. better, & having finished the 1st vol.- flattered herself she had got through the worst ...'

The Prince Regent and his librarian, and Emma

Even before *Mansfield Park* was published, Jane started her next book, *Emma*, on 21 January 1814 – 'I am going to take a heroine whom no one but myself will much like' – she told her family. The Surrey setting, and especially the visit to Box Hill, was probably inspired by Jane's knowledge of Great Bookham, where her godfather Revd Samuel Cooke was the vicar, as there are several references in her letters to visiting the Cookes there. Family tradition recorded that the fictional Highbury was based upon Leatherhead in Surrey, the nearest small town to Great Bookham, and Mrs Goddard's school in Highbury sounds remarkably like the Abbey House in Reading. There were no problems in composition, and the manuscript was finished on 29 March 1815. Later in the year Jane went to London to stay with Henry while he negotiated publication on her behalf, and this time it was offered to John Murray of Albemarle Street, who agreed to publish 2,000 copies on commission, and also undertook to publish a second edition of *Mansfield Park*, which Egerton had earlier refused to do.

While Jane was in London Henry fell ill, and as his wife Eliza had died in 1813, Jane stayed on for several weeks longer than originally intended to nurse her brother. Dr Matthew Baillie, one of Henry's doctors, was also a court physician and attended the Prince Regent. Jane's authorship was by now an open secret in London – largely due to Henry's own proud acknowledgement of his sister's name whenever he heard her books referred to in society – and Dr Baillie told Jane one day '... that the Prince was a great admirer of her novels; that he often read them, and had a set in each of his residences – That *he*, the physician, had told his Royal Highness that Miss Austen was now in London, and that by the Prince's desire, Mr. Clarke, the Librarian of Carlton House, would speedily wait upon her'. The Librarian was the

Jane Austen

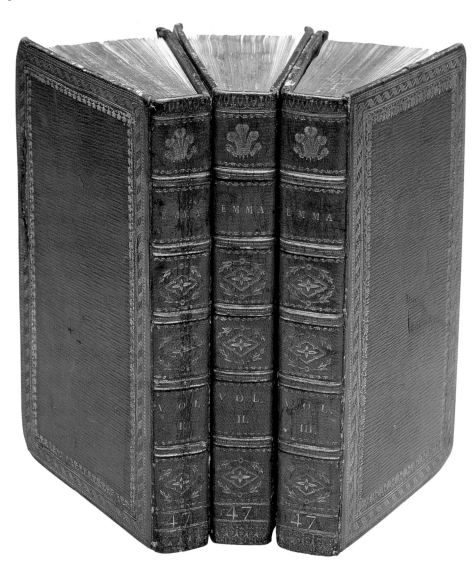

The specially bound copy
of Emma, *sent to the
Prince Regent, via
Revd Dr. James Stanier
Clarke, in
December 1815.*

The Royal Library,
Windsor Castle.

View of Box Hill, Surrey;
by George Lambert, 1743.

Tate Gallery, London

Revd James Stanier Clarke, who called at Henry's house, reiterated the previous compliments, 'adding many civilities as to the pleasure his Royal Highness had received from her novels', and invited Jane to see the library at the Prince Regent's small but luxurious London palace. She went there on 13 November, and in the course of this visit 'Mr. Clarke, speaking again of the Regent's admiration of her writing, declared himself charged to say, that if Miss Austen had any other novel forthcoming, she was quite at liberty to dedicate it to the Prince'. Jane in fact thoroughly disapproved of the Prince Regent's extravagant and immoral lifestyle, but as it was obvious that a dedication was indeed expected, this was added to *Emma* and a copy of the work, specially bound in red morocco gilt, was sent to Carlton House in mid-December, a few days prior to general publication.

Emma received several favourable reviews in the ensuing months of 1816 and sold well; unfortunately the second edition of *Mansfield Park* was not in demand, and the losses Murray made on this venture had to be offset against the profits of *Emma*, so Jane's net gain was barely £40 and that not received until early in 1817. As in the case of *Mansfield Park*, Jane kept her own private list of 'Opinions of Emma', recording her family's considered comments as to how they ranked it for enjoyment compared with her earlier works. Of her friends' opinions, one of the Kentish circle 'preferred it to all the others', while the amiable but foolish Mrs Digweed in Alton said she 'did not like it so well as the others, in fact if she had not known the Author, could hardly have got through it'. The deceptively simple domestic story also puzzled other readers – the novelist Maria Edgeworth was indeed totally bewildered by it: 'There was no story in it, except that Miss Emma found that the man whom she designed for Harriet's lover was an admirer of her own – & he was affronted at being refused by Emma & Harriet wore the willow – and *smooth, thin water-gruel* is according to Emma's father's opinion a very good thing & it is very difficult to make a cook understand what you mean by *smooth thin water gruel!!*'

Last compositions

Jane had already started *Persuasion* in August 1815, and into this went her memories of her recent life in Bath, the holidays at Lyme Regis in 1803 and 1804, and the post-war situation of 1814 when the demobilised Royal Navy officers such as her own brothers – and the fictional Admiral Croft and Captain Wentworth – were trying to buy estates with their prize-money and settle back into civilian life. This novel, short as it was (only sufficient to make two volumes in publication, instead of the three or more that were customary at the time), gave Jane some problems in the final dénouement, and she had to write a second version of the closing chapters before she was satisfied. She also seems to have been slightly surprised by the independent way in which her creation of Anne Elliot had developed a life of her own, and wrote to her niece Fanny Knight: 'You may *perhaps* like the Heroine, as she is almost too good for me.'

It was probably in 1816 that Henry, acting on Jane's behalf, bought back the manuscript of *Susan* from Crosby & Co. The head of the firm, Richard Crosby, who had snubbed Jane so rudely in 1809, was 'very willing to receive back his money, and to resign all claim to the copyright. When the bargain was concluded and the money paid, but not till then, the negotiator had the satisfaction of informing him that the work which had been so lightly esteemed was by the author of "Pride and Prejudice"' – so Henry reported to Jane's first biographer. Jane intended to offer her youthful work elsewhere for publication, and so checked through it once again, changing the heroine's name to Catherine (another firm had published an anonymous two-volume novel in 1809, also called *Susan*), and writing a preface to apologise if readers now thought the story a little old-fashioned: '... thirteen years have passed since it was finished, many more since it was begun, and that during that period, places, manners, books, and opinions have undergone considerable changes'. However, perhaps writing this preface discouraged Jane herself even as she did so, for early in 1817 she told Fanny: 'Miss Catherine is put upon the Shelve for the present, and I do not know that she will ever come out'.

The very last of Jane's compositions is the opening of what seems to have been intended for another full-length comedy novel, though she wrote no more than twelve chapters before her terminal illness overtook her. It is now known to us as *Sanditon*, and concerns the potential development of the little fishing village of that name, on the coast of Sussex, into a holiday resort – or at least, such is the plan of the enthusiastic local landowner, Mr Parker, who is sinking his finances into the venture. The smart topical names of 'Trafalgar House' and 'Waterloo Crescent'

Bath, Belmont.
'Are you going as high
as Belmont? Are you
going near Camden-
place? Because if you
are, I shall have no
scruple in asking you to
take my place, and give
Anne your arm to her
father's door.' -
Persuasion

Opposite:

*Caroline Austen
(1805-80) as a child;
sketch by
Cassandra Austen,
c.1815?*

Private collection.

which he bestows upon his buildings have their counterparts in Worthing and Ramsgate, as Jane would know; and it seems likely that a trip to the Isle of Wight was also going to come into the story, based either upon information from Frank regarding his sojourn in Yarmouth, or possibly some visit Jane herself may have made to the island while she was living in Southampton. She began to write *Sanditon* on 27 January 1817, but laid the manuscript aside for the last time on 18 March of that year.

The importance of Aunts

Between 1809 and 1817 James's three children – Anna, James Edward and Caroline – often came from Steventon to stay at the Cottage, and it is to them that we owe many of the first-hand recorded memories of Jane. Caroline (born 1805) recalled: 'My visits to Chawton were frequent – I cannot tell *when* they began – they were very pleasant to me – and Aunt Jane was the great charm – As a very little girl, I was always creeping up to her, and following her whenever I could, in the house and out of it – I might not have remembered this, but for the recollection of my mother's telling me privately, I must not be troublesome to my aunt – Her charm to children was great sweetness of manner – she seemed to love you, and you loved her naturally in return – *This* as well as I can now recollect and analyse, was what I felt in my earliest days, before I was old enough to be amused by her cleverness – But soon came the delight of her playful talk – *Everything* she could make amusing to a child – Then, as I got older, and when cousins [Frank's and Charles's children] came to share the entertainment, she would tell us the most delightful stories chiefly of Fairyland, and her Fairies had all characters of their own – The tale was invented, I am sure, at the moment, and was sometimes continued for 2 or 3 days, if occasion served –'

Memories of this period of Jane's life were recorded in later years by someone outside the Austen family, the teenager Charlotte-Maria Middleton, one of the daughters of Edward's tenant at the Great House: 'I remember her as a tall thin *spare* person, with very high cheek bones great colour – sparkling Eyes not large but joyous & intelligent ... her keen sense of humour I quite remember, it oozed out very much in Mr. Bennet's Style ... We saw her often, She was a most kind & enjoyable person *to Children* but somewhat stiff & cold to strangers, She used to sit at Table at Dinner parties without uttering much probably collecting matter for her charming novels which in those days we knew nothing about – her Sister Cassandra was very lady-like but *very prim*, but my remembrance of Jane is that of her entering into all Childrens Games & liking her extremely. – We were often asked to meet her young nephews & nieces [and] were *at Chawton with them*'.

Anna Austen married Ben Lefroy of Ashe in the autumn of 1814 and had her first baby a year later, and at the end of October 1815 Jane wrote to little Caroline: 'I am sorry that you got wet in your ride; Now that you are become an Aunt, you are a person of some consequence & must excite great Interest whatever You do. I have always maintained the importance of Aunts as much as possible, & I am sure of your doing the same now'.

Jane did not see so much of the Godmersham children as of the other nephews and nieces living nearer to hand, but wrote often to her eldest niece Fanny, who was now beginning to suffer pangs of doubt concerning the depth of her attachment to her first suitor, Mr John Plumptre. She put these doubts to Jane in the autumn of 1814, and kept ever afterwards the two long, kind, considered replies Jane sent: '... I had no suspicion of any change in your feelings, and I have no scruple in saying that you cannot be in Love ... I did consider you as being attached in a degree – quite sufficiently for happiness, as I had no doubt it would increase with opportunity ... But you certainly are not at all – there is no concealing it – Poor dear Mr J.P.! – Oh! dear Fanny, your mistake has been one that thousands of women fall into.   He was the *first* young Man who

Anna Lefroy as a young wife, c.1815.

94

attached himself to you. That was the charm, & most powerful it is. ... Anything is to be preferred or endured rather than marrying without Affection ...nothing can be compared to the misery of being bound *without* Love ...'

'So fine a Brush'

It is once again thanks largely to the Steventon children that we have some insight into Jane's method of creative composition, and the care with which she planned the plot, characters and background of her fiction. In 1814 Anna embarked upon a novel, and offered the chapters one by one to her aunt for discussion and criticism. She kept the five letters she received in reply, and these demonstrate Jane's self-imposed standards of meticulous attention to detail in order to create an entirely accurate and credible work of fiction, and the way in which her personal experiences were remembered and used as background: 'I am not sensible of any Blunders about Dawlish. The Library was particularly pitiful & wretched 12 years ago, & not likely to have anybody's publication ...Lyme will not do. Lyme is towards 40 miles distance from Dawlish & would not be talked of there ... They must be *two* days going from Dawlish to Bath; they are nearly 100 miles apart ... And we think you had better not leave England. Let the Portmans go to Ireland, but as you know nothing of the Manners there you had better not go with them. You will be in danger of giving false representations. Stick to Bath & the Foresters. There you will be quite at home. ...We are not satisfied with Mrs. F's settling herself as Tenant & near neighbour to such a Man as Sir T.H. ... A woman, going with two girls just growing up, into a Neighbourhood where she knows nobody but one Man, of not very good character, is an awkwardness which so prudent a woman as Mrs. F. would not be likely to fall into. Remember, she is very prudent;- you must not let her act inconsistently ... You are now collecting your People delightfully, getting them exactly into such a spot as is the delight of my life;- 3 or 4 Families in a Country

Fanny Knight aged 12; watercolour sketch made by Cassandra Austen on 3 September 1805.

Jane Austen Memorial Trust

James Edward Austen-Leigh (1798-1874), as a young clergyman, c.1825.

Private collection

Village is the very thing to work on ... What can you do with Egerton to increase the interest for him? I wish you cd. contrive something, some family occurrence to draw out his good qualities more ... I would not seriously recommend anything Improbable, but if you cd. invent something spirited for him, it wd. have a good effect.'

Two years later James Edward, in his last term at Winchester College and looking forward to going up to Oxford within a few months, also started writing a novel, which he read aloud to his grandmother and aunts whenever he visited the Cottage. A letter from Mary Lloyd prompted Jane to reply to him: '... I am quite concerned for the loss your Mother mentions in her Letter; two Chapters & a half to be missing is monstrous! It is well that *I* have not been at Steventon lately, & therefore cannot be suspected of purloining them;- two strong twigs & a half towards a Nest of my own, would have been something. – I do not think however that any theft of that sort would be really very useful to me. What should I do with your strong, manly, spirited Sketches, full of Variety and Glow? – How could I possibly join them on to the little bit (two Inches wide) of Ivory on which I work with so fine a Brush, as produces little effect after much labour?'

It was also in 1816 that Jane heard again from the Prince Regent's librarian, Revd James Stanier Clarke; after her visit to Carlton House the previous year he had suggested she should write a novel with a clergyman as the hero – indeed, sketching out the plot for her, with a hero whose career remarkably resembled his own – and he now wrote to point out that, as the Prince Regent's daughter Princess Charlotte had just become engaged to Prince Leopold of Saxe-Cobourg, '... any historical

Chawton

Jane's manuscript for
the first version of the
ending of Persuasion.

The British Library,
Egerton MS 3038. folio 1.

Chap. 10.

With all this knowledge of Mr E—
& with this ~~authority~~ to impart it—
Anne ~~quitted~~ Westgate Build^{gs}—her
mind deeply busy in reviewing what she
had heard, feeling, thinking, recalling
& foreseeing everything; shocked at ~~about~~
~~the Elliots~~, sighing over future, ~~rejoiced~~
~~grieved for Lady Russell.~~ ~~—~~

[several heavily crossed-out lines]

had been entire.— ~~And~~ The Embarrassment which must be felt from their ~~nearer~~
~~meeting~~ in his presence!— How to behave to him.—how to get rid of him?—
What to do by any of the Party at
home?—where to be blind? where
to be active?—It was altogether a
confusion of Images & Doubts—a
perplexity, an agitation ~~Embarrassment~~ which
she could not see the end of. —
And She was in Gay St—& still so
much ~~far~~ engrossed, ~~as to~~ ~~start~~ that she started on being
addressed by Adml Croft, as if he were a
person unlikely to be met there.

romance, illustrative of the history of the august House of Cobourg, would just now be very interesting'. To this kind but entirely inappropriate suggestion Jane replied with her carefully considered self-assessment: 'You are very very kind in your hints as to the sort of composition which might recommend me at present, and I am fully sensible that an historical romance, founded on the House of Saxe Cobourg, might be much more to the purpose of profit or popularity than such pictures of domestic life in country villages as I deal in. But I could no more write a romance than an epic poem. I could not sit seriously down to write a serious romance under any other motive than to save my life; and if it were indispensable for me to keep it up and never relax into laughing at myself or other people, I am sure I should be hung before I had finished the first chapter. No, I must keep to my own style and go on in my own way; and though I may never succeed again in that, I am convinced that I should totally fail in any other'.

Terminal illness

Early in 1816 Jane's health began to give way, and in recent years medical opinion has suggested that, based on her own description of her symptoms, she had fallen victim to the then unrecognised Addison's Disease. This is a form of kidney failure, sometimes caused by a tubercular infection, which eventually proves fatal. There are periods of remission during which the patient feels much better and is hopeful of recovery, but crises occur during periods of mental stress. The years 1814-16 had indeed been worrying for the Austens: Edward Knight was attacked in a lawsuit by distant connections of the original Knight family who were laying claim to his Chawton estate and the threat of dispossession hung over him for years; and apart from Henry Austen's dangerous illness in 1815, his banking partnerships failed in the difficult economic conditions of the post-war years and he was declared bankrupt in the spring of 1816. Various members of the family lost the money they had deposited with him – though luckily for Jane, she had already invested most of her earnings safely. As Mrs Austen and her daughters were so dependent upon support from her sons, anything which reduced their incomes would cast a shadow upon the future of the little group at the Cottage. A further disappointment occurred in the spring of 1817, when Mr Leigh-Perrot died and left everything to his wife for her lifetime, with his sister and her family to share his property only at that uncertain future date.

Cassandra took Jane to Cheltenham in the spring of 1816 to drink the spa waters, which were supposed to be 'singularly efficacious in all bilious complaints', but during the next few months she grew gradually weaker. She had difficulty in completing the current work, *Persuasion*, as her family remembered; she thought her original idea for the ending was 'tame and flat, and was desirous of producing something better. This weighed upon her mind, the more so probably on account of the weak state of her health; so that one night she retired to rest in very low spirits. But such depression was little in accordance with her nature, and was soon shaken off. The next morning she awoke to more cheerful views and brighter inspirations: the sense of power revived; and imagination resumed its course...' The 'tame and flat' original ending was short and rather unconvincing: Admiral Croft meets Anne in the street and invites her back to his lodgings to call on his wife, but to her embarrassment she finds Captain Wentworth is also there. He tells her that the Crofts have heard she is engaged to Mr. Elliot and will therefore wish to return to live at Kellynch, and when Anne denies this rumour Wentworth immediately proposes to her. Jane's 'brighter inspirations' produced the revised setting of the busy family party at the White Hart, which gives the time and space for Wentworth to overhear Anne's discussion with Captain Harville regarding the emotional differences between men and women, and her heartfelt cry: 'All the privilege I claim for my own sex (it is not a very enviable one, you need not covet it) is that of loving longest, when existence or when hope is gone...' that encourages him to write his repentant letter begging her to forgive him and renew their long-broken engagement.

One of the periods of remission occurred in the New Year of 1817 and Jane felt well enough to start *Sanditon*, but her ailment soon reappeared and a few weeks later a more severe attack of fever caused her to cease composition for ever. The local apothecary, Mr Curtis of Alton, admitted his inability to help her further, and the family decided that Jane should go to Winchester to consult the much-respected Mr Lyford of the County Hospital there. A sad little party – Cassandra and Jane, in a carriage lent by James, and with Henry and Edward's undergraduate son William

riding beside – arrived at No 8 College Street, Winchester, on the rainy afternoon of 24 May. Jane wrote to James Edward in a tone of resolute and wryly humourous optimism: 'Our Lodgings are very comfortable. We have a neat little Drawing room with a Bow-window overlooking Dr Gabell's garden ... Mr Lyford says he will cure me, & if he fails I shall draw up a Memorial and lay it before the Dean & Chapter, & have no doubt of redress from that Pious, Learned, and Disinterested Body'. Privately, however, Mr Lyford told the family that his patient's case was desperate and that Jane could not survive much longer. She lingered a few more weeks, cheerful to the last, but the final crisis occurred on the evening of 17 July, as Cassandra later wrote to Fanny Knight: 'She felt herself to be dying about half an hour before she became tranquil and apparently unconscious. ... she said she could not tell us what she sufferd, tho' she complaind of little fixed pain. When I asked her if there was any thing she wanted, her answer was she wanted nothing but death & some of her words were "God grant me patience, Pray for me oh Pray for me."' She died peacefully in Cassandra's arms in the dawn hours of 18 July 1817.

In Memory of
JANE AUSTEN,
youngeſt daughter of the late
Revᵈ GEORGE AUSTEN,
formerly Rector of Steventon in this County
ſhe departed this Life on the 18ᵗʰ of July 1817,
aged 41, after a long illneſs ſupported with
the patience and the hopes of a Chriſtian,

The benevolence of her heart,
the ſweetneſs of her temper, and
the extraordinary endowments of her mind
obtained the regard of all who knew her, and
the warmeſt love of her intimate connections.

Their grief is in proportion to their affection
they know their loſs to be irreparable,
but in their deepeſt affliction they are confoled
by a firm though humble hope that her charity,
devotion, faith and purity, have rendered
her ſoul acceptable in the ſight of her
REDEEMER.

*Winchester Cathedral;
Jane's ledger stone in
the north aisle.
The inscription was
composed by
Henry Austen.*

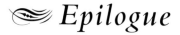 *Epilogue*

Posthumous publication

Jane was buried in the north aisle of Winchester Cathedral on 24 July, and her grave is marked by a plain black slab, with the inscription upon it composed by Henry; later in the nineteenth century her nephew Revd James Edward Austen-Leigh arranged for a memorial brass plaque to be placed on the nearby wall.

Henry Austen took over his sister's last two manuscripts and in the autumn of 1817 arranged with John Murray for their publication together in four volumes, which appeared just at the beginning of 1818. It was apparently he who entitled them *Northanger Abbey* and *Persuasion*, as it seems to have been Jane's practice to write her stories first and choose titles for them only when she was finally satisfied with the completion and polishing of her texts.

Manuscripts

No complete manuscript of any of the six novels survives — presumably once they had safely appeared in print Jane threw away her working copies. Cassandra kept until her own death in 1845 the three volumes of the *Juvenilia*, the fair copy of the short novel *Lady Susan*, the abortive beginning of *The Watsons*, the unfinished *Sanditon*, and the cancelled chapters of *Persuasion*, as well as a number of Jane's letters and some other miscellaneous items. These were distributed by her amongst her brothers and their families, and over the ensuing years most have entered the collections of libraries in either the United Kingdom or United States, by sale or gift. The Pierpont Morgan Library in New York owns the bulk of Jane's letters, as well as the fair copy of *Lady Susan* and part of *The Watsons* manuscript; the Bodleian Library in Oxford has Volume the First of the *Juvenilia*; King's College, Cambridge has *Sanditon*; and the British Library owns Volume the Second and Volume the Third of the *Juvenilia*, as well as the *Persuasion* chapters, the 'Opinions' of *Mansfield Park* and of *Emma*, and about a dozen of the letters. Other letters and manuscripts are more widely scattered around the world, some still remaining in private hands.

NORTHANGER ABBEY:

AND

PERSUASION.

Miss Austen

BY THE AUTHOR OF " PRIDE AND PREJUDICE,"
" MANSFIELD-PARK," &C.

WITH A BIOGRAPHICAL NOTICE OF THE
AUTHOR.

IN FOUR VOLUMES.

VOL. I.

LONDON:

JOHN MURRAY, ALBEMARLE-STREET.

1818.

*Title-page of the first
edition of*
Northanger Abbey
and Persuasion,
*1818. An early
reader has inserted
'Miss Austen' as the
author's name.*

*The British Library
Cup. 403. BB.13.*

When the new British Library building at St. Pancras, London, was being erected in the 1990s, the hoarding surrounding the site was decorated with portraits of famous people in British history. Jane Austen is shown here, next to the great railway engineer Isambard Kingdom Brunel.

'I write only for Fame'

In her letter of 14 January 1796 to Cassandra, and long before any question of publication was envisaged, Jane said jokingly: 'I am very much flattered by your commendation of my last Letter, for I write only for Fame and without any view to pecuniary Emolument —' This is indeed a case of a true word being spoken in jest, for her books have never been out of print since they were first published. Although they may seem at first reading to be no more than undramatic stories of ordinary young men and women falling in love, it is the importance of this event in anyone's life which gives them their perennial popularity. Second and subsequent readings gradually reveal the depth of Jane's literary skill and instinctive understanding of the vagaries of human nature in the way she creates her characters by deft touches of dialogue and authorial comment until they step off the page as living individuals. Her creative genius cannot be better summed up than in the words of one of her earliest readers, who wrote to Fanny Knight: 'A great many thanks for the loan of *Emma*, which I am delighted with. I like it better than any. Every character is thoroughly kept up. ... Miss Bates is incomparable, but I was nearly killed with those precious treasures! They are Unique, & really with more fun than I can express. I am at Highbury all day, & I can't help feeling I have just got into a new set of acquaintance. No one writes such good sense & so very comfortable'.

Manydown Wednesday Feb: 11th

My dear Cassandra

As I have no Mr. Smithson to write of I can date my letters. — Yours to my Mother has been forwarded to me this morning, with a request that I would take on me the office of acknowledging it. I should not however have thought it necessary to write so soon, but for the arrival of a letter from Charles to myself. It was written last Saturday from off the Start, & conveyed to Popham Lane by Captn. Boyle in his way to Midgham. He came from Lisbon in the Endymion, & I will copy Charles' account of his conjectures about Frank. — "He has not seen my brother lately, nor does he expect to find him arrived, as he met Capt: Inglis at Rhodes going up to take command of the Petterel as he was coming down, but supposes he will arrive in less than a fortnight from this time, in some ship which is expected to reach England about that time with dispatches from Sir Ralph Abercrombie." — The event must shew what sort of a Conjuror Capt: Boyle is. — The Endymion has

Letter from Jane to Cassandra, 11 February 1801.

The British Library, Add. MS.41253.A, f.1.

Chawton Great House.
Early twentieth century

JANE AUSTEN 1775 – 1817

❧ *Chronology*

1764   April 26

Marriage of Revd George Austen and Cassandra Leigh; they go to live at Deane, Hampshire, and their first three children — James, George, and Edward — are born there.

1768   Summer.

The Austen family move to Steventon, and five more children — Henry, Cassandra, Francis, Jane, and Charles — are born there during the next few years.

1773   March 23

Mr. Austen becomes Rector of Deane as well as Steventon, and takes pupils at Steventon from now until 1796.

1775   December 16

Jane Austen born at Steventon.

1781   Jane's cousin, Eliza Hancock, marries Jean-François Capot de Feuillide, in France.

1782   First mention of Jane in family tradition, and the first of the family's amateur theatrical productions takes place.

1783   Jane's third brother, Edward, is adopted by Mr. and Mrs. Thomas Knight II, and begins to spend time with them at Godmersham in Kent.

Jane, with her elder sister Cassandra and cousin Jane Cooper, goes to school for some months in Oxford and then Southampton.

1785   Spring.

Jane and Cassandra go to the Abbey House school in Reading.

1786   April.

Jane's fifth brother Francis goes to the Royal Naval Academy, Portsmouth.

December.

Jane and Cassandra have left school and are at home again in Steventon.

Between now and 1793 Jane writes her *Juvenilia*.

1788   Summer.

Mr. and Mrs. Austen take Jane and Cassandra on a trip to Kent and London.

1791   July.

Jane's sixth and youngest brother Charles goes to the Royal Naval Academy, Portsmouth.

December 27

Edward Austen marries Elizabeth Bridges, and they live at Rowling in Kent.

1792   March 27

Jane's eldest brother James marries Anne Mathew.

Winter

Cassandra becomes engaged to Revd Tom Fowle.

1793   January 21

Louis XVI of France is guillotined.

January 23

Edward Austen's first child, Fanny, born at Rowling.

February 1

Republican France declares war on Great Britain and Holland.

April 8

Jane's fourth brother Henry becomes a lieutenant in the Oxfordshire Militia.

April 15

James Austen's first child, Anna, born at Deane.

June 3

Jane writes the last item of her *Juvenilia*.

1794   February 22

M. de Feuillide guillotined in Paris.

Autumn

Jane possibly writes the novella *Lady Susan* this year.

1795   Jane probably writes *Elinor and Marianne* this year.

May 3

James's wife Anne dies, and infant Anna is sent to live at Steventon Rectory.

Autumn.

Revd Tom Fowle joins Lord Craven as his private chaplain for the West Indian campaign.

December.

Tom Lefroy visits Ashe Rectory — he and Jane have a flirtation over the Christmas holiday period.

1796 October.

Jane starts writing *First Impressions*.

1797 January 17

James Austen marries Mary Lloyd, and infant Anna returns to live at Deane.

February.

Revd Tom Fowle dies of fever at San Domingo and is buried at sea.

August.

Jane finishes *First Impressions*; Mr. Austen offers it to publisher Cadell in London, but it is rejected sight unseen.

November

Jane starts converting *Elinor and Marianne* into *Sense and Sensibility*.

Mrs. Austen takes her daughters to visit Mr. and Mrs. Leigh-Perrot in Bath.

Edward Austen and his young family move from Rowling to Godmersham.

December 31

Henry Austen marries his cousin, the widowed Eliza de Feuillide, in London.

1798 Jane probably starts writing *Susan* (later to become *Northanger Abbey*).

November 17

James Austen's son James-Edward born at Deane.

1799 Summer.

Jane probably finishes *Susan* (*Northanger Abbey*) about now.

August 14

Mrs. Leigh-Perrot charged with shoplifting and committed to Ilchester Gaol.

1800   March 29

Mrs. Leigh-Perrot tried at Taunton and acquitted.

December

Mr. Austen decides to retire and move to Bath.

1801   January 24

Henry Austen resigns his commission in the Oxfordshire Militia and sets up as a banker and Army agent in London.

May

The Austen family leave Steventon for Bath, and then go for a seaside holiday in the West Country. Jane's traditionary West Country romance presumably occurs between now and the autumn of 1804.

1802   March 25

Peace of Amiens concludes the war with France.

Summer

Charles Austen joins his family for a seaside holiday in the West Country, and possibly also in Wales.

December

Jane and Cassandra visit James and Mary at Steventon; while there, Harris Bigg-Wither proposes to Jane and she accepts him, only to withdraw her consent the following day, and she returns to Bath immediately.

Winter

Jane revises *Susan (Northanger Abbey)*.

1803   Spring

Jane sells *Susan (Northanger Abbey)* to publisher Crosby; he promises to publish it by 1804, but does not do so.

May 18

Napoleon breaks the Peace of Amiens, and war with France recommences.

Summer

The Austens visit Ramsgate in Kent, and possibly also go to the West Country again.

November

The Austens visit Lyme Regis.

1804   Jane probably starts writing *The Watsons* this year, but leaves it unfinished.

Summer

The Austens visit Lyme Regis again.

1805   January 21

Mr. Austen dies and is buried in Bath.

Summer

Martha Lloyd joins forces with Mrs. Austen and her daughters.

June 18

James Austen's younger daughter Caroline born at Steventon.

October 21

Battle of Trafalgar.

1806   July 2

Mrs. Austen and her daughters finally leave Bath; they visit Clifton, Adlestrop, Stoneleigh and Hamstall Ridware, before settling in Southampton in the autumn.

July 24

Francis Austen marries Mary Gibson.

1807   May 19

Charles Austen marries Fanny Palmer, in Bermuda.

1808   October 10

Edward Austen's wife Elizabeth dies at Godmersham.

1809   April 5

Jane makes an unsuccessful attempt to secure the publication of *Susan* (*Northanger Abbey*).

July 7

Mrs. Austen and her daughters, and Martha Lloyd, move to Chawton, Hants.

1810   Winter

Sense and Sensibility is accepted for publication by Egerton.

1811   February

Jane starts planning *Mansfield Park*.

October 30

Sense and Sensibility published.

Winter

Jane starts revising *First Impressions* into *Pride and Prejudice*.

1812   June 17

America declares war on Great Britain.

October 14

Mrs. Thomas Knight II dies, and Edward Austen now officially takes name of Knight.

Autumn

Jane sells copyright of *Pride and Prejudice* to Egerton.

1813   January 28

Pride and Prejudice published. Jane half-way through *Mansfield Park*.

July

Jane finishes *Mansfield Park*.

November

Mansfield Park accepted for publication by Egerton probably about now.

1814   January 21

Jane commences *Emma*.

April 5

Napoleon abdicates and is exiled to Elba.

May 9

Mansfield Park published.

December 24

Treaty of Ghent officially ends war with America.

1815   March

Napoleon escapes and resumes power in France; hostilities recommence.

March 29

Emma finished.

June 18

Battle of Waterloo finally ends war with France.

August 8

Jane starts *Persuasion*.

October 4

Henry Austen takes Jane to London; he falls ill, and she stays longer than anticipated.

November 13

Jane visits Carlton House, and receives an invitation to dedicate a future work to the Prince Regent.

December

Emma published by Murray, and dedicated to the Prince Regent.

1816 Spring

Jane's health begins to fail. Henry Austen buys back MS of *Susan* (*Northanger Abbey*), which Jane revises and intends to offer again for publication.

July 18

First draft of *Persuasion* finished.

August 6

Persuasion finally completed.

1817 January 27

Jane starts *Sanditon*.

March 18

Jane now too ill to work, and has to leave *Sanditon* unfinished.

May 24

Cassandra takes Jane to Winchester for medical attention.

July 18

Jane dies in the early morning.

July 24

Buried in Winchester Cathedral.

December

Northanger Abbey and *Persuasion* published together by Murray, with 'Biographical Notice' added by Henry Austen.

Epilogue

1870   Jane's nephew, Revd James-Edward Austen-Leigh, published his *Memoir of Jane Austen*, from which all subsequent biographies have stemmed.

1871   Mr. Austen-Leigh published a second and enlarged edition of his *Memoir*, including in this the short story *Lady Susan*, the cancelled chapters of *Persuasion*, and the unfinished *The Watsons*.

1884   Jane's great-nephew, Lord Brabourne, published *Letters of Jane Austen*, the first attempt to collect her surviving correspondence.

1922   Volume the Second of the *Juvenilia* published.

1925   The manuscript of the unfinished *Sanditon* published in full.

1932   Dr. R.W.Chapman published *Jane Austen's Letters to her sister Cassandra and others*, giving letters unknown to Lord Brabourne.

1933   Volume the First of the *Juvenilia* published.

1951   Volume the Third of the *Juvenilia* published.

1952   Second edition of Dr. Chapman's *Jane Austen's Letters* published, with additions.

1954   Dr. Chapman published *Jane Austen's Minor Works*, which included the three volumes of *Juvenilia* and other smaller items.

1980   B. C. Southam published *Jane Austen's 'Sir Charles Grandison'*, a small manuscript discovered in 1977.

1995   Deirdre Le Faye published the third (new) edition of *Jane Austen's Letters*, containing further additions to the Chapman collections.

⚉ *Further Reading*

The Novels

The definitive edition of Jane Austen's novels is that published by the Oxford University Press in six volumes, with useful notes, essays and period illustrations.   This edition was first prepared in the 1920s, but has been reprinted at intervals ever since.

Penguin Books (Harmondsworth, Middx) keep paperback editions constantly in print, and these have notes and good introductions to each text.

The Letters

Le Faye, Deirdre (ed.): *Jane Austen's Letters* (OUP, 1995, and paperback 1997).

Biographies and reminiscences

Austen, Caroline: *My Aunt Jane Austen* (Jane Austen Society, Chawton, 1952 and later reprint).

—: *Reminiscences* (Jane Austen Society, Chawton, 1986).

Austen-Leigh, James Edward: *A Memoir of Jane Austen* (London, 1870, and later reprints).

Austen-Leigh, W. & R.A., and Le Faye, Deirdre: *Jane Austen: A Family Record* (The British Library, London, 1989, and paperback 1993).

Cecil, David: *A Portrait of Jane Austen* (Constable & Co, London, 1978 and later reprints).

Jenkins, Elizabeth: *Jane Austen: a Life* (Victor Gollancz Ltd, London, 1938 and later reprints).

Selwyn, David (ed.): *Collected Poems & Verse of the Austen Family* (Carcanet Press, Manchester, 1996).

Tucker, George Holbert: *A Goodly Heritage: a history of Jane Austen's Family* (Carcanet Press, Manchester, 1983; and reprinted in paperback as *A History of Jane Austen's Family* (Sutton Publishing, Gloucester, 1998).

Social history and biography

Batey, Mavis: *Jane Austen and the English Landscape* (Barn Elms Publishing, London, 1996).

Black, Maggie, and Le Faye, Deirdre: *The Jane Austen Cookbook* (British Museum Press, London, 1995).

Collins, Irene: *Jane Austen and the Clergy* (The Hambledon Press, London, 1993).

Copeland, Dr Edward: *Women Writing About Money* (CUP, 1995).

Lane, Maggie: *Jane Austen and Food* (The Hambledon Press, London, 1995).

Nicolson, Nigel: *The World of Jane Austen* (Weidenfeld & Nicolson, London, 1991).

Aids to study

Copeland, E., & McMaster, J. (eds): *The Cambridge Companion to Jane Austen* (CUP, 1997).

Grey, J. David (ed): *The Jane Austen Handbook* (The Athlone Press, London, 1986).

Pinion, F.B.: *A Jane Austen Companion* (Macmillan Press Ltd, London, 1973).

Film and television

Birtwistle, S., & Conklin, S.: *The Making of Pride & Prejudice* (Penguin Books, Harmondsworth, Middx, 1995).

Birtwistle, S., & Conklin, S.: *The Making of Jane Austen's Emma* (Penguin Books, Harmondsworth, Middx, 1996).

Thompson, Emma: *Jane Austen's Sense & Sensibility: screenplay & diaries* (Bloomsbury Publishing plc, London, 1995).

Opposite:
Title page of
'The History of England'
from Volume the Second
of the Juvenilia

The British Library
Add. MS. 59874, f.77

The History of England
from the reign of
Henry the 4th
to the death of
Charles the 1st

By a partial, prejudiced, & ignorant Historian.

To Miss Austen eldest daughter of the Revd.
George Austen, this work is inscribed with
all due respect by

The Author

N.B. There will be very few Dates in
this History.

Index

The British Library is grateful to the following for permission to reproduce illustrations: Joan Austen-Leigh; the Jane Austen Memorial Trust; Willis Museum, Basingstoke; Victoria Art Gallery, Bath; Royal Museum and Art Gallery, Canterbury; Jarrold Publications; the National Maritime Musem, London; the Trustees of the National Portrait Gallery, London; Philpot Museum, Lyme Regis; Portsmouth City Art Gallery; Portsmouth City Museum; the Museum of Reading; the Rector and Churchwardens of Steventon Parish; St John's College, Oxford; the Tate Gallery, London; Winchester Cathedral Library; and the Royal Library, Windsor Castle.

Front cover illustrations: Watercolour sketch of Jane Austen by her sister Cassandra, probably made around 1810 (National Portrait Gallery, London); page from '*Volume the Third*', addressed to 'Miss Austen' and signed 'The Author', Steventon, August, 1792 (British Library Add. MS 65381, f.16v); a Scene in Leigh Woods, *c.*1822 by Francis Danby (City of Bristol Museum and Art Gallery).

Back cover illustrations: Watercolour sketch of Jane Austen, made by Cassandra in the summer of 1804 (Private Collection); view of Chawton Cottage (Jane Austen Memorial Trust).

Text © 1998 Deirdre Le Faye

Illustrations © 1998 The British Library Board and other named copyright owners

Published in the United States of America by
Oxford University Press, Inc.
198 Madison Avenue
New York
NY 10016

Oxford is a registered trademark of Oxford University Press, Inc.

ISBN 0-19-521440-4

First published 1998 by
The British Library
96 Euston Road
London NW1 2DB

Maps by John Mitchell
Designed and typeset by Crayon Design, Stoke Row, Henley on Thames
Origination by Crayon Design and Grafiscan, Verona
Printed in Italy by Artegrafica